VOICE & STYLE

BY

JOHNNY PAYNE

WRITER'S DIGEST BOOKS
CINCINNATI, OHIO

*This book is dedicated to my
creative writing students,
and to Miriam, Sonja and Clayton.*

ABOUT THE AUTHOR

Johnny Payne is the author of the novel *Kentuckiana,* the novella *The Ambassador's Son,* numerous short stories, a collection of essays entitled *Conquest of the New Word* and other books. His musical play, *The Devil in Disputanta,* has been performed on stage and radio in Chicago and will be produced at Barter Theater in Abingdon, Virginia. He has also done extensive work as an ethnographer and a translator. Johnny Payne teaches creative writing at Northwestern University.

Voice and Style. Copyright © 1995 by Johnny Payne. Printed and bound in the United States of America. All rights reserved. No part of this book may be reproduced in any form or by any electronic or mechanical means including information storage and retrieval systems without permission in writing from the publisher, except by a reviewer, who may quote brief passages in a review. Published by Writer's Digest Books, an imprint of F&W Publications, Inc., 1507 Dana Avenue, Cincinnati, Ohio 45207. (800)289-0963. First edition.

This hardcover edition of *Voice & Style* features a "self-jacket" that eliminates the need for a separate dust jacket. It provides sturdy protection for your book while it saves paper, trees and energy.
Other fine Writer's Digest Books are available from your local bookstore or direct from the publisher.

99 98 97 96 95   5 4 3 2 1

Library of Congress Cataloging-in-Publication Data

Payne, Johnny.
    Voice & style / Johnny Payne.—1st ed.
        p.   cm.—(The elements of fiction writing)
    Includes index.
    ISBN 0-89879-693-8 (alk. paper)
    1. Fiction—Authorship.   2. Style, Literary.   I. Title.   II. Series.
  PN3355.P368   1995
  808.3—dc20
                                    95-32394
                                       CIP

Edited by Jack Heffron
Designed by Angela Lennert

CONTENTS

Introduction • *1*

PART I: THE NARRATIVE VOICE

   1. Habits of Speech • *8*

   2. Authority and Voice • *29*

   3. Atmosphere and Tonc • *52*

PART II: THE DRAMATIC VOICE

   4. The Voice in Dialogue • *74*

   5. Dialect and Voice • *98*

PART III: THE AUTHORIAL VOICE

   6. Defining the Subject • *119*

   7. The Influence of Other Voices • *141*

PART IV: VOICE AND STYLE

   8. Many Voices, One Voice • *164*

INTRODUCTION

Voice is the key element in fiction, the one which, in effect, contains and shapes all the other elements of the story. Style is the voice's means of expression. Plot, characterization, setting, theme, dialogue—all of these pieces exist in isolation unless voice makes them into active principles and brings them together. The common misperception sees voice for an author as what "screen presence" is to an actor—some mysterious quality that you either have or you don't. But voice, like all elements of fiction, requires an appreciable dimension of technique. While the writer often wishes to create the illusion of the voice telling the tale as effortless and natural, the discriminating author knows how much careful calculation has gone into producing an unforgettable character or authorial voice that lingers in the reader's ear long after the book is closed. That voice, more than any other element, seduces the reader into going back to the shelf to read another book by the same author.

The "aura" of voice can be broken down into components of style and analyzed, and it can also be cultivated through careful attention to the writing of other authors, followed by sophisticated forms of imitation, and then the creation of one's own voice. The goal of this cultivated awareness of the many voices available to you, is to allow you to draw on the full repertoire of style that exists within literary traditions. In addition, coming to understand the dramatic, narrative and authorial aspects of voice will help you control the layers of voice that, in a story, have to function in concert if the supreme sleight of

1

hand of a "single voice" is to be successful.

We only need to proceed a couple of sentences into certain novels to hear the unmistakable voice that will be guiding us through it, and to begin to understand not only what it means to say to us, but how. The narrator of Jane Austen's *Emma* sounds, from the outset, self-possessed and stately, and whatever contretemps Emma must live through in the course of the novel, the voice isn't going to get ruffled telling about them.

> Emma Woodhouse, handsome, clever, and rich, with a comfortable home and happy disposition, seemed to unite some of the best blessings of existence, and had lived nearly twenty-one years in the world with very little to distress or vex her.

In Robert Penn Warren's *All the King's Men*, on the other hand, the narrator jump-starts the novel with the first words uttered in caps, clueing you in that if you're going to keep up with this story, you're going to have to expend plenty of adrenaline along the whole route, spilling out of you like gasoline through a ripped chassis.

> MASON CITY.
> To get there you follow Highway 58, going northeast out of the city, and it is a good highway and new. Or was new. You look up the highway and it is straight for miles, coming at you, with the black line down the center coming at and at you, black and slick and tarry-shining against the white of the slab, and the heat dazzles up from the white slab so that only the black line is clear, coming at you with the whine of the tires, and if you don't quit staring at that line and don't take a few deep breaths and slap yourself hard on the back of the neck you'll hypnotize yourself and you'll come to just at the moment when the right front wheel hooks over into the black dirt shoulder off the slab, and you'll try to jerk her back on but you can't because the slab is high like a curb, and maybe you'll try to reach to turn off the ignition just as she starts the dive. But you won't make it, of course.

Warren addresses you directly, with none of the discreet obeisance and observance of Austen's implied etiquette between reader and author. One voice is staid and reflective, the other urgent and visceral; one voice amusing and detached, the other guttural with black humor.

No new plots exist, strictly speaking. When all is said and done, plot serves, as it did in Aristotle's definition of it, largely as a story's set of structuring devices—neither more nor less. "Plotting" simply means mapping. Given this fact, there is nothing inherently exciting about plot, especially plot that exists only for its own manic sake. If plot does not get urged on by a persuasive authorial voice, no amount of hairpin twists and turns will make it lively. Plotting then becomes plodding. In the movies, there are only so many ways you can stage a car chase, no matter how many explosives you have to work with. In fiction, there are only so many ways you can have a character decide to leave home or commit adultery. And that character, no matter how colorful or interesting he may seem to you, will move no one if he doesn't possess a credible, or better yet riveting, character voice.

The dialogue, no matter how ingenious, will sound like mere words strung together if it is not guided, colored and subtly commented on by the narrative voice. The words of a screenplay can depend upon the visual images provided by the camera, the vision of the director, and the actual speaking intonation of the actors to make it spectacular. Printed fiction has nothing to depend on, ultimately, but voice, in its authorial, narrative and dramatic aspects. Therein lies our sole spectacle.

If a writer doesn't learn to use the capability of voice with skill, dialogue and description will read as a pale imitation of a screenplay, without any of the "production values" that cinema and live theater depend on. The writer of fiction, therefore, must cultivate and master that essence particular to fiction's domain. Voice, in the sense that I will speak of it in the pages ahead, is better suited to fiction than to any other medium. It is what makes fiction continue to occupy a unique place in the arts, in an age in which electronic media might otherwise usurp its role. That prospect should excite us.

I have drawn on a wide range of modern and contemporary fiction writers from the United States, Western and Central Europe, Russia, South Africa and Latin America, in providing examples for various aspects of technique. No single style predominates or is given preferential treatment. I do not assume realism, for instance, as a "norm" that all other styles relate to in an inferior relation. I treat style as not only a technical concept, but, by implication, as a historical one. Realism coexists alongside fantastical tales; metafiction and absurd satire alongside tender, muted and poetic prose. I believe that one of the marks of the mature, or maturing, fiction writer is her willingness to assume different guises, to slip into different voices and styles to test the limits of her ambition.

To assume the existence of your voice beforehand, rather than working to arrive at it, cuts you off at the beginning from the possibility of developing range and scope. Despite this book's title, you won't hear me speaking much about refining and tuning your voicebox. I think of style as a repertoire, and not as a mysterious quality that cannot be fathomed. The abundance of examples provided in each chapter allows you to grasp in a concrete way the methods and principles offered. In some cases, I use my own fiction and drama as examples, to allow you to see me working, as it were, from the inside out. My understanding of voice and style derives in large part from the countless hours I have spent writing. I do, however, set limits on this didactic borrowing of my own creative prose. Insofar as I do cite it, I try to use it evenhandedly, as illustration for a given point about technique, and to give some evidence that I try to practice what I preach. For the most part, I give attention to my favorite authors, the ones whose books I'm always placing in the hands of my students and friends, when they ask me to recommend a well-written novel or story.

If I'm personal and playful and opinionated in these eight chapters as well as analytical and methodical, that's because writing a textbook or a manual gives one no excuse to be boring. Describing concepts as ineffable and elusive as voice and style calls one's entire being into play and one's sense of play into being—fair play and foul play alike. Mischief and serious purpose coexist in most of us. No less here.

In chapter one, you're given instruction in how to lend minor characters a greater presence in the story, and how to establish key characters quickly through the habits of speech you lend them. These habits of speech, which differ somewhat from the issue of dialect (taken up in chapter five), work by conveying an intense, vivid impression in a short time. Even the briefest of scenes, monologues or tales can possess the quality of fullness we tend to associate with longer works. Mastering habits of speech teaches you to work by compression, to turn in a tight space.

Chapter two, in its discussion of the relation of voice to point of view, raises the crucial question of narrative authority. Who is ultimately responsible for the information imparted by the story? Whose vision prevails and conditions our understanding of the material? Depending on how reliable or unreliable you make the narrative voice, or the amount and quality of irony you invest in it, that answer will vary wildly. Where aspects of voice are concerned, there is no more important decision you can make than the point of view you select for your prose. Point of view acts as a kind of efficient cause in fiction. It sets everything in motion.

Chapter three introduces you to atmosphere and tone. These subtle qualities of voice, far from evanescent, make the setting of your fiction live and pulse, rather than sit on the page in angular type like a petrified forest. Atmosphere and tone transform the setting into an occasion for the development of your characters. Atmosphere does not exist for its own sake. It lets a reader grasp in a tangible way how the characters perceive and inhabit their fictional world.

Chapter four situates the dramatic voice within the context of dialogue. You will begin to think of dialogue not only as "speech," but as an indirect form of description, and as a way of playing character voice off the narrative point of view. In its own way dialogue, as an aspect of voice, can sometimes substitute for certain other elements of fiction. At the least, dialogue can wrap itself around those elements like the serpent winding itself around Eve's leg as it hisses seduction at her ever so softly and sinuously.

Chapter five puts its emphasis on that specialized form of voice known as dialect. Cultivating dialect in the proper way, as a selective representation of a voice's essence, rather than as a phonetic parlor game, allows your character voices to be both regional (or neighborhood) and personal. You don't have to hail from the country to use dialect. Everybody knows some or has heard some. This chapter also takes up some notions about the mechanics of style and the relation of voice to grammar.

The business of chapter six is to face head-on the sometime nemesis of most fiction writers—finding a proper subject, so that he can begin to write. Although the task of writing can feel daunting, there is no such thing as writer's block. Almost everyone has plenty to write about. To help you feel your way toward that store of subjects that exists within you, waiting to be tapped, I suggest ways to discover the story's primary voice. Once that primary voice gets established, the subject at times will almost begin to write itself. In any event, the primary voice serves to define the subject with greater clarity.

Another frequent source of both inspiration and confusion for beginning writers—the so-called "anxiety of influence"— gets its due in chapter seven. I see influence as an inexhaustible source rather than a weight. By taking the discovery of voice out of the realm of a strictly inner pursuit, and turning it into a systematic and public pursuit of some of the hundreds upon hundreds of voices available to us within literature, influence and imitation become usable concepts.

Finally, chapter eight discusses ways for you to combine the three levels of voice—dramatic, narrative and authorial— brought forth in the first seven chapters. After you have begun to comprehend the essentials of each aspect of voice separately, combining them for more far-reaching and simultaneous effects will seem not only possible, but downright appealing.

Each chapter ends with a series of exercises in style to be written out. Each exercise is keyed to the discussion of a specific writer (or at times, a couple of writers) within that same chapter. The exercises are suggestive rather than restrictive. Rereading the section pertaining to a particular exercise, after you've read the entire chapter, will help you fix in your mind how to proceed with that specific writing task.

Perform the exercises one by one, and give yourself sufficient time between exercises to appreciate what you've wrought. For some people, this time could be a day or two, for others a week or more. Even reading straight through the book without completing the exercises would, I hope, prove entertaining and give you insight into how to read fiction with a high level of concentration (the first step in the writing process). But this book is meant to be taken in stages, and meant above all to enable your creative process. For this reason, I suggest you consume it a chapter or two at a time.

Take heart. Writing is hard, but it ain't that hard. The method contained in these pages has evolved out of my ongoing engagement over years as a creative writing teacher. I've watched a sizeable number of pretty inexperienced writers, and many with no previous experience whatsoever, develop into proficient, sometimes inspired and inspiring makers of fiction. If I believe anything about the relation between art and knowledge, I passionately believe that creative writing can be taught. I hope that by the time you finish this book, you'll believe it too.

CHAPTER 1

HABITS OF SPEECH

HABITS OF SPEECH ALLOW A WRITER to put characters onto the page quickly. A habit of speech is a distinctive way of talking, although it should not be confused with dialect. Dialect is a character's overall style of talking. Habits of speech are the locutions, the specific memorable and suitable phrases, that give even minor characters a presence in the story. The speech of a character can never be considered wholly apart from the description used to characterize him. I will always recall the phrase of a young man I knew for a brief period in Albuquerque, where I worked as a substitute mathematics teacher. In a short time, he made an impression, and though I've never seen him since, his image floats into my mind from time to time.

He was a crack student in my algebra class, diligent, on the quiet side, but with a palpable intensity about him. Sinewy and lean, sixteen years old, with deep-set eyes and long hair parted on the side, he sported a wispy set of whiskers, and looked vaguely Italian. One afternoon after class, he lingered, and I began to find out more about him. His name was Paul, and his accent was New York, from the Bronx, if memory serves me. He turned out to be a mechanic as well as a student. He and his father and several of his innumerable brothers had opened a repair shop on the north side of the city, out one of those half-deserted roads dotted with windowless aluminum shacks and roadside marquees that advertised massages. At the time, I was driving a Korean War jeep that continually leaked oil from some invisible internal hemorrhage that no one had been able

to find. Paul told me he would find it, and that I should bring
the jeep by his repair shop at my convenience.

A few days later, I did. The shop was set on a couple of acres
of arid land where the extended family had built a ramshackle
compound of sorts, girded about with chicken wire. Chickens
wandered to and fro on the property, searching mostly in vain
for a stray grain of feed on the desolate grounds among the
tumbleweeds and thickets of brush. I found Paul seated in the
garage on a bench, working on a disassembled carburetor. He
was slow in movement, a slow talker, a lord of flatbushes and
flatbeds, and he brought to the task of being a mechanic an
uncanny quiet and concentration. No sense of frustration
showed in his work habits. Every piece would find its place
within the machinery sooner or later. It couldn't be rushed. He
brought a similar calm deliberation to his solving of quadratic
equations in my classroom. His grasp of them was almost instan-
taneous, but he nonetheless solved them slowly, as if he didn't
want the pleasure to end too soon.

Looking up from the bits of metal on his workbench, he
acknowledged my presence with a flicker of his piercing eyes
and an easy but cryptic smile. "Brought the jeep?"

"Yeah, it's outside."

"Good. I'll get to it." Reaching over, he picked up a mari-
juana cigarette burning in an ashtray, and took a long slow toke
off of it. Closing his eyes to relish the sensation, he then ex-
haled. Paul looked at me again, and in his dreamy, slow-motion
Bronx, spoke a single sentence that has been ringing in my ears
ever since. "You know," he said, "if it wasn't for math, you
wouldn't be here."

He didn't elaborate any further on the remark—simply
asked me to have a seat and went back to the carburetor. I
never knew whether he was just making an obvious remark to
indicate that my having taken a job as a math teacher was my
reason for being in Albuquerque and meeting him. Or whether
Paul, like some Wittgenstein or Descartes in greasy overalls, had
been silently working out a mathematical proof of our collective
existence. For all I knew, this inscrutable sixteen-year-old whiz
kid and owner of a roadside business, was a backwater genius.

He did fix my jeep, though I never quite caught the explanation of what was wrong with it. As in his working of geometry problems, he took shortcuts that didn't follow the steps set out by the textbook. You either had to take his word for it or not; all he offered was the finished result. After that I moved, so I never had a chance to find out for sure what he meant by his remark. More than once I've thought about making him a central character in a book or play, except that I can't imagine him possessing much more than that one line of dialogue—"If it wasn't for math, you wouldn't be here." In the meantime, he remains as my Rosencrantz or Guildenstern, occupying a minor role on the page, but nonetheless vivid for that fact. As long as a character's habits of speech are well observed, a few lines of dialogue and a few details are sufficient for creating as intense an impression as you might like. Dialect is the sound that remains in your ear after you have forgotten the content of what has been said. A habit of speech is more the single overheard phrase you go around repeating for weeks on end, because the content of it stayed with you.

SHARING THE HUCKLEBERRY PIE

The novelist Teresa Porzecanski, whose novels tend to be short, specializes in establishing her characters in a brief space. Even the process that brought me to her work is littered with people who came and went, leaving their peculiar locutions hanging in the air.

After over a year of correspondence and telephone calls with an Argentine writer, whose novel I badly wanted to bring over into English, I learned I could not secure the translation rights, and had to give up the project. He called me long distance, his booming voice crackling with static, waking me up at six in the morning, to say "Johnny, the sample translation you sent me was brilliant. Just brilliant. Here is my agent's telephone number in New York. I also want us to start a correspondence between author and translator right away, and write brilliant letters to each other, which we'll also publish. I'll write you either from Paris or Buenos Aires. Brilliant, I tell you."

Then he disappeared for months, and I'd call his agent, a nervous Latina who was just learning her trade and who seemed to walk around in a state of perpetual bewilderment, as though she'd misplaced her keys right before an urgent appointment. She'd say, in an almost pleading tone of voice, "I don't know where Ricardo is. If you find out, let me know, will you?" When I finally tracked him down, he thundered "Johnny Payne! Ah, yes. Remind me who you are." I said, "Never mind. Forget about it. I'll write you when you get to Paris."

By this time, I was experiencing what in Spanish they call *hastío*. I was fed up with all the energy I'd expended in vain. Then, in a matter of a few days, I went from first discovering Teresa Porzecanski's work to becoming her friend and translator. Someone had given me a catalog of new fiction from Latin America, and the blurb in it on Porzecanski's writing caught my eye, so I went to the library to see if it had any of her work available. It did, and I was immediately engrossed by the sophistication and variety of her style—the range of diction and thought, abstract and sensual at the same time; the syntax, tortuous but somehow remarkably fluid. She had a keen anthropological mind, and the texture of her language seemed to me as rough, porous and tactile as a weathered stone icon. I sat down and translated a couple of her very short pieces as finger exercises.

Two days later I received, out of the blue, a flyer announcing that she was coming to my school as part of a half-day conference. I was happy. When I called up the conference organizer to express my surprise and wonder that Teresa Porzecanski happened to be coming all the way from Uruguay for a half-day conference, she seemed underwhelmed. In the jaded, world-weary voice so often sported by twenty-five-year-old graduate students, she said "No. She's coming from Davis. It's only seventy miles from here."

In a few minutes I was on the phone with Porzecanski, who explained she'd taken up residence in Davis, California for a couple of months, doing anthropological research, and that I should come up to see her. I jumped in my Toyota and drove up to interview her and show her my fresh translations, still warm from the computer printer.

I prepared myself in my mind for meeting this preternaturally humble luminary of modern fiction. Strangely, though, a person I remember equally well from that day is a cashier I saw for less than five minutes. When I arrived in Davis, I stopped in a bakery to buy a pie, so I wouldn't arrive empty-handed. I pointed to one with purple juice oozing through the crust, and asked what it was. "That's huckleberry pie," said the cashier. "You never had huckleberry pie?" I shook my head. He was incredulous. "This man never had huckleberry pie," he announced to the bakery at large, shaking his own head in wonder. "This is the absolute best pie you're *ever* gonna eat."

And it was. Sharing that pie with an intensely freckled Uruguayan with the unlikely last name Porzecanski in an inexplicable way remedied all the frustrations I had gone through with her Argentine counterpart from the Río de la Plata. What made me savor the experience doubly was the cashier's prophecy. His habit of speech stayed on my lips, a huckleberry stain that I never managed to remove. He is a minor character in my story, true, but not a forgettable one. His habit of speech allows one to infer the kind of character he might become if more dialogue were added. One assumes that the kinds of things he'd have to say would be of a piece with the single phrase above— good natured, full of vitality, showing a willingness to be intimate with total strangers. When you create a minor character, you should try to convey a clear sense of what is essential about him or her, as if you really could go on for pages about that character if you wished.

ABBREVIATED SPEECH

Porzecanski excels at putting the myriad characters who populate her novels into the stream of the story in short order. In her 1994 *Perfumes de Cartago* (Perfumes of Carthage), set in Montevideo in the 1930s, one of the characters, the widower

Alegre Carmona, feels jealous of the adulterous perfume maker Jeremías Berro. Berro has refused permission for Carmona to wed Berro's sister-in-law, and in one scene of the novel, the frustrated Carmona goes to a rabbi to unburden himself. Carmona waits in the anteroom, his tension building as he wonders whether the rabbi will receive him. Porzecanski allows the scene—an interlude, and the only scene in which the rabbi appears—to discharge itself with relative speed.

> "Let him come in," he finally heard the Rabbi say to his wife. She returned with a pale face and a diminutive smile. Carmona followed her, afraid to make too much noise on the plank floor. He entered into a shaded room, where a silhouette traced itself against the white light of the small window. On all sides, bookshelves seemed to grow from floor to ceiling branching out like live matter. The Rabbi coughed from deep within the cavity of his belly and invited him to sit down.
>
> There was an awkward silence. Carmona didn't know how to begin speaking and everything he might say seemed to him elemental. "How does one explain," he at last got out with difficulty, "cruelty? That is to say, Rabbi, the evil of those who walk this earth without being punished, without fear of God, without any proper sense of things?" And at once he repented of having said it, as if whatever he might say had already been answered a thousand and one times in other places.
>
> The Rabbi offered a broad smile, of surprisingly beautiful teeth, and his eyes narrowed as their shine increased.
>
> "Come on, my friend, cough up what you're carrying inside. Nothing better than finding words to name what's happening to us. There is that God who moves us, who confounds us, but who makes us grow. Amen. And let's drink to our health," said the Rabbi as he served up red wine in two short cups of opaque glass.

Porzecanski doesn't spend an inordinate amount of time setting the scene. Instead, she conveys Carmona's discomfort through the way he enters the room and feels cloistered by the "live matter" of the bookshelves, whose organic, Talmudic wisdom he has come to seek yet also fears. We don't spend any more time in the anteroom than is needed to have him ushered to the study. The Rabbi, in short, is in. Hatred has been festering in Carmona's heart so long that it has become oppressive, and he wants to be rid of it as much as if he had an abscessed tooth.

Thus, it is both psychologically accurate and efficient in terms of fictional technique to have him simply blurt out his burning query: "How does one explain cruelty?" The big philosophical questions, the kind uttered by Job, sound ridiculous and small coming from our own mouths, and yet they are the ones we most want the answers to. Instantly, Carmona wants to retract his utterance, but it is too late. He has let loose an irretrievable confession, and an irreplaceable habit of speech, as much a part of Carmona as his shop assistant's stutter is a part of him. A stutter is more audible, but this man's rash way of putting things qualifies as no less idiosyncratic or distinctive than a stutter would be. There he stands, discovered before the Rabbi, and before us, his readers. Alegre Carmona's habit of speech announces itself—lurching, fitful, hesitant. Though he goes on afterward at modest length to explain his brief against Jeremías Berro, his very first sentence of this encounter is characteristic, and serves to define him.

The Rabbi Nissim Alfieh's answer likewise does the same for him. Everything about the Rabbi suggests a character quite opposite that of Carmona. He is expansive, comfortable in his forthrightness, as inclined to forgive as to castigate. His habit of speech is an invitation rather than a confession. "Come on, my friend, cough up what you're carrying inside." He proceeds to offer Alegre Carmona a parable, and the parting advice that "It is better for my enemy to see my happiness than for me to see his misfortune." Porzecanski allows him abbreviated forms of speech such as maxims, parables and anecdotes, that in lesser hands could make the Rabbi appear preachy and Polonius-like in the dispensing of cheap advice.

But by tethering this character's habits of speech to his dramatic function as a frayed but genuine holy man in the story, she is able to make the Rabbi seem an affable and comprehending sort, unafraid to draw on the wisdom of the centuries. He doesn't mind that his proverbs sound a bit secondhand. If they were good enough for the ancestors, shouldn't they be good enough for us? Having been used many times, so that they have become familiar, for him doesn't rob them of any of their power to instruct. The author's tactic of interspersing sayings with spontaneous conversation also allows Porzecanski to create the Rabbi fully in the short space of four pages. The two men share the same dialect, more or less, but their habits of speech couldn't be more different.

THE FOLK MONOLOGUE

Another version of this use of folk sayings appears in Jamaica Kincaid's brief story-monologue "Girl," set on the Caribbean island of Antigua. The narrator is obviously the Girl's mother, and from the outset, she looks in the mood to reel off some mighty advice. The monologue is stylized. Rather than covering a realistic span of time, Kincaid offers a compressed version of the Mother's sayings that have filled the girl's ears for years.

> Wash the white clothes on Monday and put them on the stone heap; wash the color clothes on Tuesday and put them on the clothesline to dry; don't walk barehead in the hot sun; cook pumpkin fritters in very hot sweet oil; soak your little clothes right after you take them off . . . always eat your food in such a way that it won't turn someone else's stomach; on Sundays try to walk like a lady and not like the slut you are so bent on becoming; don't sing benna in Sunday school . . .

By no accident, the story continues on in this vein, comprising a single grammatical sentence written in a highly vernacular style. This character's habit of speech is lecturing, colorful, stern, peppered with the specific taboos and requirements of being a woman in Antigua. Kincaid can offer a full-blown portrait of a segment of this society by choosing representative bits of information, and encasing them within a particular, memorable style of communication. In accomplishing this task, she takes the folk tale as her model.

Folk tales are usually conservative in nature, in terms of the social function they fulfill. By conservative I mean that they tend to support the status quo, the values that allow a given form of society and its traditions to remain intact. In Kincaid's story, the precise way women wash and iron clothes, the way they choose and prepare food, the mores for how to court and how to marry, get passed on from mother to daughter. These mores require that the daughter perform these tasks in just the same way her mother did. The mother's voice, stern, repeatedly refers to the daughter as "the slut I know you are bent on becoming," as she attempts to cajole her daughter into conforming to the strict rules of social behavior (i.e., not singing benna in church).

However, folk tales can also be subversive or self-contradictory, and sometimes slyly impart to the listener ways of getting around the strict rules of behavior set down. Folk wisdom is only useful and durable to the extent that it can actually and realistically be incorporated into the lives of its adherents. Here, the mother's moralistic tone is belied by some of the specific advice she gives to the daughter in the latter part of the monologue. Her advice to the daughter on how to "throw back a fish you don't like," "this is how you bully a man; this is how a man bullies you," reveals a submerged compassion on the mother's part. Kincaid's aphoristic clauses suggest, at first, that the mother is no more or less than the mouthpiece for a set of petrified platitudes, harsh and inflexible. But this is not so, as the reader realizes when the advice starts to take on other overtones.

Thus, the use of proverbs and maxims to achieve urgency doesn't necessarily weaken an author's ability to achieve a more telescoped, but equally complex development of a character. Artistically, this method is as viable as any other. The idea the mother conveys to the daughter is: "I'm a woman too, I've been through the things you're going to have to deal with, and here are some of the secret tricks known among our women for dealing with the adversities of our lot.''

She even gives her advice on how to perform an abortion, which seems odd in light of her exhortations about not "becoming a slut.'' The mother is a steely-eyed realist, and tacitly acknowledges the fact that the daughter will have a love life anyway. In the end, she seems more to side with the daughter than with the community the daughter is a part of: "this is how to love a man, and if this doesn't work there are other ways, and if they don't work don't feel too bad about giving up.''

The final sentence issues a challenge to the daughter not to be so meek and compliant. The "girl" referred to in the title will only become a woman once she learns the wiles for getting around all the restrictions put on her behavior by society. One can imagine her at some future date, speaking to her own daughter in the same steely, reprimanding voice as the narrator. One can say that Kincaid uses the same device for the mother as Porzecanski does in her portrayal of the Rabbi. But the particular habit of speech of each character clearly distinguishes one "proverbial" talker from the other.

Be liberal in putting common phrases in the mouths of your characters. There's a difference between clichéd language and language that is simply vernacular or familiar. Once you weave those familiar phrases into a style of speech, they will lend your tale a believable texture. A sparkling prose style is laudable, but don't feel that you have to dole out elegant diction to all characters. Let some of them be plainspoken.

DESCRIPTION AND DIALOGUE

The habits of speech to which I've been referring don't have to take the form of straight dialogue. As we've seen, Jamaica Kincaid, in her brief tale, makes the "speaking" character into a first-person narrator, and thereby changes what might otherwise be thought of as speech or dialogue into the story's controlling voice. In this way, what she says is not subordinated to description, because dialogue, in effect, becomes description.

One reason why first-person narrators have become so popular is that the writer is tempted by being able to render dialogue and description simultaneously, to have the description, as it were, built in. This kind of first-person narration, however, does not come particularly easy. It stands or falls on the writer's ability as a mimic, or at least on the ability to make readers believe that he is a good mimic.

It might be helpful to think of the difference in stand-up comedy, between observational humor and impersonation. Observational humor can have varying degrees of success, even if we recognize and respond to only parts of what the comic is describing. When it comes to impersonations, the comic has to be dead on. Even a couple of degrees of inaccuracy, and nobody laughs. The excellent mimic creates the illusion of ease, without disclosing the months of careful study that go into producing a calculated effect.

Unless you, as a writer, are endowed with a tremendously perceptive natural ear, a reliance on the pure immediacy of a firsthand narrative voice always carries a risk. A combination of description and dialogue, on the other hand, allows you to compensate for any deficiencies in your natural ear, and not have to throw in your lot with sheer voice. That, after all, is what technique serves for. If a person's natural abilities in this area are prodigious, there's no need for training. Otherwise, it becomes necessary to do something besides performing a tour de force of character voice.

CHARACTER STATUS: MAJOR AND MINOR

The difference between these two tacks is not insignificant. I am ultimately talking about the question of the character's status within the story, and how that status is determined by how much rein the designated voice allows it to have. Here, we return to the issue of major and minor characters. Giving the speaking voice lots of space and many pages will certainly lend it a quantitative primacy within the story you're writing, but doesn't guarantee by itself that the character or narrator will hold anyone's attention.

Conversely, it is quite possible to have a character speak her piece adequately within a very short space, as long as you have provided her with the appropriate forum or vehicle for doing so. Indeed, "minor" characters possess virtues all their own, ones that aren't always available to major characters.

A model for achieving this effect of compression presents itself in "Little Miracles, Kept Promises," by Sandra Cisneros. She uses as the implied conceit of this story, a visit to the shrines of various saints one finds in Hispanic culture, and the folk device of letters written to saints or to God asking for help or expressing thanks—thus the story's title. Part of what makes "Little Miracles" so effective is Cisneros's decision to give all the "minor" characters an equal status, so that they end up becoming, in their aggregate, a collective protagonist of sorts. They end up doing what none of them could do by themselves.

In the first three-quarters of the story, a series of notes to the saints are simply presented, without any commentary or framing voice. Each character's defining habit of speech takes the form of a few terse lines or, at most, a few paragraphs. This method temporarily exalts each of the written notes, giving it central status within the story for the short time that it occupies center stage. Each "character," though halfway anonymous, for all practical purposes usurps the narrator's or protagonist's role, and our attention stays fully trained, albeit for an instant, on that character's idiosyncratic prayer or complaint. These texts are directed toward sacred beings, but are vernacular in the language they use. Also, as I have said, their scale remains small, like horoscopes, fortunes or personal ads.

A powerful series of verbal flashes results, ranging in tone from gently satirical to heartbreaking, as we glimpse these characters trying to recuperate from their daily woes and catastrophes, praying for "little miracles" or giving thanks for the ones they have received.

Dear San Antonio de Padua,
    Can you please help me find a man who isn't a pain

in the nalgas. There aren't any in Texas, I swear. Especially not in San Antonio.

Can you do something about all the educated Chicanos who have to go to California to find a job. I guess what my sister Irma says is true: "If you didn't get a husband when you were in college, you don't get one.". . .

Can you send me a man man? I mean someone who's not ashamed to be seen cooking or cleaning or looking after himself . . . In other words, don't send me someone like my brothers who my mother ruined with too much chichi, or I'll throw him back . . .

> Ms. Barbara Ybañez
> San Antonio, TX

Miraculous Black Christ of Esquipulas,

Please make our grandson to be nice to us and stay away from drugs. Save him to find a job and move away from us. Thank you.

> Grandma y Grandfather
> Harlingen

Jesus Christ,

Please keep Deborah Abrego and Ralph S. Urrea together forever.

> Love,
> Deborah Abrego
> Sabinal, Texas

Here, voice controls the other elements of fiction, but without residing in a single character. Cisneros largely disperses the plot throughout the story, because nobody's individual life tale, according to the rules set up by "Little Miracles," has an exclusive claim on our attention. Likewise, character remains at a remove, since the narrative structure forces us to fill in the gaps and details inevitably left by the partial information a short note can provide. Sketchy, yet intimate. Anonymous, yet as personal as one can get when speaking one's innermost thoughts to a saint in a time of sorrow or relief. Deborah Abrego's "lover's complaint" is reminiscent of the adolescent graffiti found painted on rocks and trees—a cliché, yet a strangely moving one in its perenially naive hopefulness.

Cisneros accomplishes this sympathy because of the immediacy of these voices, their nakedness, and because she leavens their mundane pleas with a certain amount of humor, such as in the letter of Ms. Barbara Ybañez, looking for "a man who isn't a pain in the nalgas," not like her brothers, "ruined with too much chichi [i.e., titty]." This bantering, knowing tone contrasts with the straightforward, earnest anxiety of the grandparents worried about their grandson's involvement with drugs.

Importantly, Cisneros doesn't let any of these characters speak for too long, with the exception of a young girl, Cisneros's alter ego, who merits a more extended monologue at the story's end, after all the other characters have spoken. If any of these letters took hold for more than a few paragraphs, it would begin to arrogate the story to itself, to disrupt the collage of voices, and end up diluting the effect of rapid-fire intimacy so carefully and delicately established. In fact, the alter ego's voice strikes me as, in some ways, the weakest of all the character voices, precisely because she gives it too much space. Cisneros's technique fits her material, given her central theme that everyone has his or her story to tell, full of heartache and unexpected small triumphs.

In the telling, she vacillates between honoring the inarticulate directness with which people pour out their longings, and mildly satirizing the humble means of expression to which most people are limited by a combination of circumstance, education and temperament. Though "Little Miracles, Kept Promises" is a highly crafted work—indeed, one of Cisneros's most expert stories—it nonetheless aspires to the status of a text that she has simply run across, rather than invented herself. Hardly any found text, however, could be so efficient in its means as this. Still, her story wants to create the impression that we have stumbled into some wayside church, and are now poring over the scrawled notes pinned beside the altar. As such, she, like Jamaica Kincaid, has to rely to a large degree on her ability to recreate diverse habits of folk speech.

VERBAL MANNERISMS

Folk speech, however, is not the only habit of speech worth mastering. The flamboyant fictionist Donald Barthelme excels at capturing the verbal mannerisms of urban sophisticates, his parodic humor sometimes tender, sometimes sharp and wicked. Barthelme's procedure consists of letting his characters go on and on about their dissatisfactions in a way that, in some respects, is banal and repetitive. At the same time, he consistently injects absurdities and dadaistic digressions into the speech of his melancholic malcontents. The brilliance of this method lies in its power to rescue his characters and their stories from the hackneyed genre of urban ennui that easily becomes precious when taken too seriously.

Barthelme understands all too well people's impatience with the protracted angst of the world-weary intelligentsia. When he delves into that subject matter, he lampoons the usual assumptions about it, by giving his protagonists a mock-earnest tone that, at the same time, is loaded with absurdist habits of speech. I remember meeting Barthelme at a writing conference, at a cocktail party filled with other writers, young and old, who aspired to make it to the place he had achieved within American letters. He had obviously "arrived," and yet something in his air suggested that he couldn't help treating the whole business of "being a writer" as a gargantuan joke, in which he himself played the biggest fool of all. A part of him clung to the simplicity of the author's task, the real struggle between writer and page, and wanted to reject all the trappings that surrounded it—the book-signing, the arty small talk, the celebrity worship, the desperate bohemianism.

Not that he acted in any way unsympathetic toward any of the conference participants. I detected, however, a slight reserve in his bearing, a refusal to fritter too much of himself away in the public persona of "being a writer"—which often doesn't have much to do with the business of writing anyway. Writing is a task, whereas being a writer is an attitude, a social posture. Donald Barthelme's long tapered beard, the missing mustache, and the impish cast of his round face made him look almost Amish. As he stood with a bourbon and soda in hand, like the distant rich uncle in some fictional fairyland, taking in the chatter swirling around him, the twinkle in his eye seemed half sympathetic and half devilish. I could see his hyperactive parodic mind already piecing together bits of dialogue for yet another of his signature vignettes.

This atmosphere—or, as a Barthelme character might improbably and pedantically state it, this "milieu"—gets featured in his story "On the Steps of the Conservatory." The premise is simple: Two women, Hilda and Maggie, stand on the steps of the Conservatory, an unnamed sanctuary of infinite prestige and snobbery. Hilda, distraught at being turned down as an applicant to the Conservatory, seeks comfort from her friend Maggie. Maggie, who belongs to the Conservatory, vacillates between expressing fake and tepid sympathy for the rejected Hilda, and getting in savage digs at her friend.

A subject of this kind could become tedious, a grade-B John Updike story, but Barthelme rescues it at the outset by treating it in wild comic fashion. The comedy derives largely from Hilda and Maggie's habits of speech. The character psychology remains realistic and believable, but expressed in registers of language and diction that Barthelme deliberately keeps inconsistent and off-balance.

   —They will never admit me to the Conservatory, I know that now.
   —You are not Conservatory material, I'm afraid. That's the plain truth of it.
   —You're not important, they told me, just remember that, you're not important, what's so important about you? What?
   —C'mon Hilda don't fret.
   —Well Maggie it's a blow.
   —When are you going to change yourself, change yourself into a loaf or a fish?
   —Christian imagery is taught at the Conservatory, also Islamic imagery and the imagery of Public Safety.
   —Red, yellow, and green circles.

  —When they told me, I got between the poles of my rickshaw and trotted heavily away.
  —The great black ironwork doors of the Conservatory barred to you forever.
  —Trotted heavily away in the direction of my house. My small, poor house.
  —C'mon Hilda don't fret.

The pompousness of the Conservatory, the idea of a select group of "artistes" gets deflated here by the deadpan tone in which the women discuss the subjects taken up by the teachers. Maggie casually inquires about Hilda's capacity to change herself into "a loaf or a fish," in that high-minded metaphorical tone that artistic types are wont to take. Christian imagery and the imagery of Public Safety (in capital letters, naturally) are spoken in the same breath, as if they were of equivalent artistic importance. Maggie's empty reassurances, "C'mon Hilda don't fret," alternate with the melodramatic, bombastic imagery of the suffering, Romantic Artist withdrawing into solitude— "When they told me, I got between the poles of my rickshaw and trotted heavily away."

  The incongruity of the word "rickshaw" in this context makes the tone of the sentence absurdly comic rather than sad. The author disinvites us to take this whole business too much to heart. To appreciate Barthelme's handling of tone here, for contrast I suggest that you have a look at Thomas Hardy's novel, *Jude the Obscure*, in which the same theme is treated in a tragic vein. That novel is deeply moving in some regards, but passages of it sound positively overwrought, almost to the point of unintentional comedy. There, an English stone laborer with intellectual aspirations is thwarted at every turn from going beyond his humble origins and becoming a professor. The novel ends with him dying in a cul-de-sac, the wall of his room symbolically communicating with the obstructing wall of the university. In his death throes, Jude hears the triumphal cries of the university graduates, oblivious to his anonymous passing.

  Barthelme, however, is not a tragedian. Wisely, he plays to his own strengths. Likewise, you ought to play to your own strengths. Some of the most successful and memorable writers are not the most broad-ranging or prodigious ones, but those who know how to cultivate what they do possess. And, as I have already suggested, to compensate for what they don't possess. Through habits of speech, Barthelme takes Hilda and Maggie's emotions of self-pity and smugness to dizzying heights.

One of the marks of Barthelme's skill as a fiction writer is that he doesn't accept the commonplace wisdom that a character's speech always has to remain consistent. The harping on "consistency" that has become a cliché in MFA workshops ignores the fact that consistency of speech, while an effective tool, remains one of the most artificial traits that a fictional character can possess. Barthelme sees no reason why a single character can't combine elegant (or mock-elegant) flights of poetry one moment with flat and tedious statements the next. He takes delight in setting up expectations, and, in the midst of a serious intellectual discussion, promptly yanking the rug out from under us. He's a cad, and wants to be. His characters strike one as promiscuous users of language, party-crashers, prevaricators, and they grab every scrap of speech they can find to stitch into their elaborate fabrications. Desperate creatures, they press into service every word they come by, like a compulsive collector of junk who can't bear to throw anything away.

After all, people don't actually talk the same way in all situations. We have an unconscious habit of adjusting our diction, slang or patterns of speech according to the social group or company we find ourselves in. Thus, Barthelme reasons, why not do it within a single conversation? This constant switching of codes itself becomes a recognizable pattern, and creates a new definition of "consistency."

I have a friend who I find singular precisely because he's one of the only people I know who *doesn't* change his register of language, regardless of whether we're shooting pool in a bar or hobnobbing with the supposed crème de la crème of our professional lives. No matter who he finds himself with, he cusses and makes self-effacing jokes without any adjustments to circumstance. He always stands out in a crowd—not because he's colorful, although he is—but rather because he's consistent. He would not do, however, as a Barthelme character. To do so, he'd have to learn to zing from poetry to pedantry to platitude, all in the space of a single paragraph.

THE OBSESSIVE, RELENTLESS VOICE

Consistency, however, clearly has its virtues as a path for following out other kinds of speech habits. I'm thinking in particular of how one creates an obsessive, relentless voice. As you continue to progress in your own fiction-making, attempting this kind of voice will hold increasing appeal for you. It consists in finding the exact note on which to pitch a first-person story, and then sustaining that voice until the last cry of the last word on the last page, which hopefully will continue to echo in the reader's ears long after she has put the story down. Ishmael in *Moby Dick*, when you get right down to it, is a Johnny-One-Note. And yet, what a note! Being able to trace out a single obsession over an extended span of pages allows a gathering power to sweep the reader along. For some tastes, this experience is the headiest one that fiction has to offer.

A connoisseur of relentless character voice can be found in the South African novelist J.M. Coetzee, and in his novel *Age of Iron*. Its protagonist, Mrs. Curren, begins by recounting how she came upon a homeless man on the very same day she was told by her doctor that she had cancer. The encounter with this insolent, bedraggled interloper marks the beginning of a curious journey in which she will discover a hard compassion within herself, as she is forced to identify her own wretchedness with that of the wretched of the earth.

The novel's vision of humanity and of South Africa would best be described as harsh and unsparing, and its ethos as one of stoicism, though its movement is also fueled by subtle undercurrents of brotherly love. This vision is conveyed, appropriately, in a first-person narrative voice in the process of learning not to pity itself, one that refuses from the outset to spare us the unpleasant details of its reality, or to offer a single drop of false consolation. Written in the form of a letter to the woman's somewhat estranged daughter, who now lives in the United States, the novel has Mrs. Curren strain to make the daughter understand the sober finality of what is now occurring in her life.

> There is an alley down the side of the garage, you may remember it, you and your friends would sometimes play there. Now it is a dead place, waste, without use, where windblown leaves pile up and rot.
> Yesterday, at the end of this alley, I came upon a house of carton boxes and plastic sheeting and a man curled up inside, a man I recognized from the streets: tall, thin, with a weathered skin and long, carious fangs, wearing a baggy gray suit and a hat with a sagging brim. He had the hat on now, sleeping with the brim folded under his ear. A derelict, one of the derelicts who hang around the parking lots on Mill Street, cadging money from shoppers, drinking under the overpass, eating out of refuse cans. One of the homeless for whom August, month of rains, is the worst month. Asleep in his box, his legs stretched out like a marionette's, his jaw agape. An unsavory smell about him: urine, sweet wine, moldy clothing, and something else too. Unclean.
> For a while, I stood staring down on him, staring and smellng. A visitor, visiting himself on me on this of all days.

Coetzee, through Mrs. Curren, is determined to make us appreciate this man Vercueil, not in spite of his unattractiveness, but in the full light of it. To accomplish this feat, he must be precise in rendering the tone taken by Mrs. Curren. Once her voice is established, there's no turning back. Part of what gives the novel such a strong drive is that Mrs. Curren, absorbed in the immediacy of her own mortality (since she has just been diagnosed), does not stand back and preach to us in an abstract and grandiose tone about poverty and the politics of South Africa. Her narrative stays relentlessly caught up in the details of her experience of being forced to befriend this pesky, infuriating, but strangely compelling, visitor. Her obsessiveness makes her recounting of his deficiencies and state of physical and emotional dry rot almost loving in the precise attention it gives to the making of their mutual catalogue of anguish.

Whatever the status of your characters, whether their role is central or a cameo, meticulous thought must be given to what habits of speech they will be allowed to call their own. As they say in the theater, there are no small parts, only small actors. But in that rarefied state of semi-permanence known as fiction, each of your characters will be going over his or her lines for a long time. We humans have the luxury of knowing that most of what we say each day will be forgotten by those who hear it. Not so with fictional characters. Therefore, especially if one of your creations is only going to have a single speech to rehearse, one soliloquy, one bit of repartee, make sure it's the right one.

Exercises

1. Think of a character who is the protagonist in a work of fiction you admire, or one that you yourself have written. Change that character into a minor character, without sacrificing any of the character "presence" that he or she had as protagonist. Put into practice in your recreation the virtues of efficiency: telescopic speech and description, aphorism, concentrated gesture.

2. Write a "folk monologue" in the manner of Jamaica Kincaid, on any subject you desire. Keep in mind her tendency to convey the passage of time in condensed form, and her use of characteristic turns of phrase to suggest recognizable habits of speech. Your monologue should not exceed three pages in length, though you should strive for the fullness of a short story.

3. Try, as Barthelme does, to create a vignette in which the characters use various registers of diction. See what you can achieve with speech that is distinctive, but not necessarily consistent. The sources of speech may be poetic, journalistic, philosophical, proverbial, cliché—whatever you like, as long as the verbal collage you end up with adds up to a single whole. Remember, a habit of speech is a pattern of speech.

4. Now write about the same subject as in number 3, but this time absolute consistency will be your goal. Create a character voice that sounds relentless and single-minded in its concerns. This voice, unlike the preceding one, should remain as "airtight" as you can make it.

CHAPTER 2

AUTHORITY
AND VOICE

HENRY JAMES, ONE OF THE NOVELISTS most responsible for developing perspectives about point of view in modern fiction, said that the essential question for fiction is "On whose authority does the story get told?" Much of the quality of voice in a short story, novella or novel will be determined by how the authority to tell that story gets delegated, so to speak. Whether or not we view one particular character as more sympathetic or trustworthy than another, how earnestly or ironically we consider the events as they unfold, to what extent we find ourselves wanting or not to go beyond the confines of a particular character's mind—all these matters depend heavily on point of view.

But point of view is not some neutral "device" that one can install in a story and expect it to operate according to instructions. To say that someone has employed a third-person point of view in his fiction doesn't tell us much about the specific consequences of that decision for the story in question. Each third person is just as different from the next as is each first person. The difference between one and the next is accounted for largely by voice.

A third-person narrator can act as the character's advocate, for instance, as E.M. Forster does with Fielding in *A Passage to India*. Forster seems to want us to accept, ultimately, a vision of understanding and forgiveness between cultures, and subtly persuades us to look kindly on Fielding, even when he makes the inevitable missteps and misperceptions of an Englishman in India. Or, as in Thomas Mann's *Death In Venice*, the third-person narrator can severely temper sympathy towards the story's protagonist by distancing herself at selected points, like someone who doesn't wish to suffer guilt by association.

Despite the fact that Aschenbach in *Death In Venice* serves as a sort of alter ego for Mann, as the figure of the artist, Mann is not above using the third person to make his supreme artist look like a silly schoolboy on account of his crush on the young Tadeusz. When Aschenbach tries to dress like a much younger man, in order to "woo" Tadeusz, he ends up appearing ludicrously vain. Yet, since that story is also a meditation on aging and death, the third-person narrating voice is as often inflected with sorrow as it is with irony. One senses Mann's elegiac sensibility bleeding through the narration at many crucial points. Even if they are somewhat invisible, strictly speaking, third-person narrators can have plenty of personality and presence in their shaping of the story.

VOICE AND IRONY

In my novella, *The Ambassador's Son,* set in Lima, Peru, I exploit the distance between the mind of the central character, Vic Featherson, and the framing third-person voice of the narrator. In spite of Vic's sophistication and high level of education, there exist ironies and complexities of his situation that he remains unaware of until near the end of the novella. Precisely because he is so intelligent, he is vulnerable to lulling himself into the false sense of security that he will be able to handle all situations that arise in the foreign culture he is visiting for only a few days. Vic has come to South America to see his mother and his father, the Peruvian ambassador. On the second day of his brief stay, his mother persuades him to assist an American couple who are trying to adopt an Indian baby from a poor woman in one of the shantytowns.

Despite his apprehension, Vic, still a law student in the U.S., reluctantly agrees to act as an unofficial legal counsel and a guide to the couple. The Thomases, who have been stymied by the legal and cultural intricacies of trying to adopt a child in another country, don't speak Spanish. One of the first ironies of the story is that Vic, to please his mother, allows himself to be thrust into the role of interpreter to the Thomases, even though he has been in the country for even less time than they have. The dramatic movement of the story is reflected in the novella's title—*The Ambassador's Son*. He remains first and last a son, and it is as a son, more than anything else, that he will live out his fate. His love for his mother, and his desire to prove his competence to his father, will lead him far over his head in the adoption case, so much so that he will end up betraying the parents whose approval he seeks.

In order for me as author to attend adequately to the intricacy of his position, and in order to do justice to the multiple layers of meaning, I am pretty much required to use the third-person point of view. It is not that this point of view is inherently "better" than the first person. In theory, all points of view offer themselves as equally available. Some, however, allow you to accomplish certain tasks better than others. Here, the use of a third-person, detached narrator permits the framing voice to speak independently from the protagonist, while preserving the reader's sense of remaining close to the protagonist, inside his mind.

At the same time, the reader may draw conclusions about the character, for instance sensing that Vic is in danger long before he realizes it himself. The narrating voice provides a more sensible and level-headed account than the character's, simply because its passions are not engaged in the flow of the action in the same way. Unlike Vic, the narrator, who is "disembodied," doesn't have anything to lose. The narrating voice doesn't have to worry about disappointing its mother and father (for it has none), nor does it have to do right by the Thomases, since it isn't "in" the story, the way that a first-person narrator would be. This narrator hovers as a virtual ghost in the vicinity of Vic, seeing what he sees, knowing what he knows, feeling what he feels, but also knowing more.

I'll demonstrate. In the opening sequence of *The Ambassador's Son*, Vic, his parents, and a friend of theirs, General Villanueva, sit in an outdoor restaurant on the coast. Vic has just arrived, not having seen his parents in a long time, and he is trying to orient himself. I have made the decision, in this first section of the novella, to use mostly dialogue to let the reader become slowly accustomed to the immediate surroundings, the characters, and their way of talking and behaving as they order their food and discuss a rumor that cholera is spreading throughout Lima.

> Have you made up some ceviche fresh this afternoon?
> Always fresh, sir. The prawns will virtually be gasping on your plate.
> How about it, Vic? You ever tried ceviche? It's raw shellfish marinated in lemon. A local delicacy.
> I don't think we ought to be offering shellfish to our son, Chuck, or eating it ourselves, if the Ministry of Health has advised people to exercise caution. Those are bottom feeders.
> The worst thing that can happen to this country right now is for a scare to start up about the seafood. None of these so-called health risks have even been confirmed yet.

In this exchange, Vic remains mostly an observer, saying little, taking in his surroundings, trying to get acclimated. Like him, we are able to listen to the character voices, getting a fix on their opinions and biases, filling ourselves in on what we don't yet know. Because of the particular importance of the narrator in this story, I have chosen to use italics (an unusual choice for me) in the places in the opening section where the narrative voice describes the action. It narrates, for instance, how the ambassador drinks liquor.

> *The ambassador downed another pisco sour as soon as the waiter set it in front of him, and the unmelted ice cubes left in the glass shone perfect as crystals of quartz. With a sigh, he let his body sprawl in the chair. He seemed to have given up the losing battle of competing with General Villanueva's erect posture.*

A number of things happen in this brief description. First, the reader receives an idea of the mixed feelings with which Vic views his father. His father bolts the liquor down so quickly that the ice doesn't even have time to melt in the glass. He is obviously under a lot of pressure as ambassador, and without Vic's saying so, we understand that he disapproves of his father's excessive drinking and his lax posture. Without even realizing he is doing so, Vic unconsciously focuses on the details of his father's drinking. It is the third-person narrator, however, who suggests to us the quality of this unconscious discomfort.

Later in the novel, Vic complains to his mother that he's worried about how much his father drinks. In this scene, however, he makes no comment. It hasn't yet dawned on him exactly what is bothering him about his father.

The advantage of the third-person narrator's use here is that Vic doesn't even have to be fully aware that he is standing in judgment of his father. His perception of the action of drinking the liquor and slouching in the chair remains largely unconscious. The man performing the action is referred to as "the ambassador," so that what the prose emphasizes is the man's official role and the emotional distance that exists between father and son. All of this information is implied without Vic having to acknowledge it to himself or to us. The effect of the passage would be quite different if the first sentence read "My father downed another pisco sour as soon as the waiter set it in front of him, and the unmelted ice cubes left in the glass shone perfect as crystals of quartz." The judgment would seem unnecessarily harsh. Instead, one is able to feel sympathy for Vic's disorientation. Unlike him, we are able to sense the powerful, unconscious drives and emotions that have been set into motion by his seeing his parents for the first time in a long time.

The other advantage of using this type of narrator is that the picture of the slouching father suggests to the reader that the ambassador has already learned what Vic has yet to learn: that at a certain point, in a foreign culture, you have to give up resisting it or believing that you can make it over in your own image. When Vic tries to help the couple adopt the baby, and fails miserably, he will arrive at the same position as his father. He will learn the lesson his father has learned. But for now, he is only dimly aware of this possibility. If Vic were the narrator, he would not be able to express that kind of sentiment, not yet having lived through the experience of failure. Expressing the sentiment through the voice of a separate narrator allows it to exist, right at the beginning of the novella, as part of the unconscious level of meaning. The reader knows it, but the protagonist has to discover it. The narrative voice, though it can sometimes be the "same" as the character voice, is always larger and more encompassing, and understands more than the character does.

CENTERS OF CONSCIOUSNESS

Regarding point of view, whatever positive effect *The Ambassador's Son* may have on its readers, I have to lay credit in large part at the feet of Henry James, who has long been my master in such matters. *The Ambassador's Son* is the most Jamesian piece of fiction I have written. The voice is my own invention, but that voice, as I have said, cannot exist separate from answering James's question "On whose authority does the story get told?" James's finest novel, in my mind, is one of his earliest, *The Portrait of a Lady*. The third person "center of consciousness," Henry James's invention, has held sway to some extent over every generation of fiction writers since then—whether they know it or not. Even his first-person narrators, because they are deliberately impersonal, tend to sound like third-person narrators.

A center of consciousness means that the narration, while third person, comes through a single focal character, usually the story's protagonist. Even though it's narrated from the outside, the center of consciousness puts the reader in a position of standing over the character's shoulder, seeing what she sees, experiencing what she experiences. The reader also is able, to a considerable extent, to get inside the character's thoughts, while feeling just detached enough to make interpretations and judgments about the character's actions, behavior, and dialogue.

James's portrayal of the undoing of the independent-minded Isabel Archer in *The Portrait of a Lady* represents a model of finesse and subtlety. James gives clear insight into the modus operandi that would become his trademark when he describes how the idea for this novel unfolded in his mind. Noting that the general tendency of authors was to reveal a character by adding up what the other characters surrounding him or her perceived and said, James rejects that path as too superficial and too scattered. He prefers to give a more distinctive, focused and complex view of the protagonist, not by making her the mouthpiece of her own actions, but by forging a third-person *voice*.

The first-person point of view does not appeal to James for Isabel Archer because it would more strictly limit him to her somewhat naive and disingenuous perceptions. She has no inkling of the corruption of the people whose company she keeps. The voice James forges, therefore, does not belong in the most exclusive sense to the protagonist herself, but instead is a "center of consciousness" that combines the intimacy of how Isabel Archer might describe herself with the sophistication and irony of how she might be perceived by those who move in a larger orbit. Yet James, in discarding the option of giving those in the inner circle the final say, is nonetheless after . . .

> . . . the view of their relation to those surrounding her. Make it predominantly a view of *their* relation and the trick is played: you give the general sense of her effect, and you give it, so far as the raising of a superstructure goes, with the maximum of ease. Well, I recall perfectly how little . . . the maximum of ease appealed to me, and how I seemed to get rid of it by an honest transposition of the weights in the two scales.

James wants to give more than a "general sense" of his protagonist. He is not satisfied with simply tracing out a set of emotional correspondences, as if they were all somehow of equal value and interest. For this reason, James, in his preface to *The Portrait of a Lady*, rejects the "easy" path.

> "Place the centre of the subject in the young woman's own consciousness," I said to myself, "and you get as interesting and as beautiful a difficulty as you could wish. Stick to *that* for the centre; put the heaviest weight in *that* scale, which will be so largely the scale of her relation to herself. Make her only interested enough, at the same time, in the things that are not herself, and this relation needn't fear to be too limited. Place meanwhile in the other scale the lighter weight (which is usually the one that tips the balance of interest): press least hard, in short, on the consciousness of your heroine's satellites, especially the male; make it an interest only contributive to the greater one . . ."

In James's "difficult" balance, Isabel is far from possessing the truth about her own situation, and yet she remains at every moment the story's central focus. She, in turn, is interested in those around her, while not fully capable of gauging their behavior. As far as point of view is concerned, she needs them to reflect and/or absorb the sunlight of her disposition from their darker surfaces. They, the "satellites," on the other hand, believe that they can fully understand and control her, but in terms of the story, they are at a decided disadvantage. They are made to remain at a certain distance, from us and from her, and we can't really penetrate their minds. Therefore, our trust is most likely to fall to Isabel, and even though her perspective is partial, we let our sympathies be guided by her consciousness. She remains the heroine. But despite our sympathy, we are constantly engaged in the activity of reading Isabel "against" herself, letting ourselves understand and anticipate what she doesn't, filling in the gaps and blind spots that the third person inevitably makes us privy to.

BEING INTENSE WITHOUT PERSPIRING

These gaps and blind spots themselves provide a rich source of dramatic action and psychological development. This was

Henry James's great insight. James wanted, as he said, to "produce the maximum of intensity with the minimum of strain." This effect is evident in a conversation Isabel has with Gilbert Osmond, the man she will eventually wed. When it is already too late, she will discover his conniving, cold-hearted nature, his manipulative designs and the pleasure he takes in frustrating others from realizing their dreams and ambitions. In the first significant conversation they have, James employs a complex ironic narrative voice to introduce the layers of misunderstanding and deceit that are to follow. Commenting on Isabel's discomfort about this new, "sophisticated" circle, the narrative voice tells us that . . .

> . . . a part of Isabel's fatigue came from the effort to appear as intelligent as she believed Madame Merle had described her, and from the fear (very unsusual for her) of exposing—not her ignorance; for that she cared comparatively little—but her possible grossness of perception. It would have annoyed her to express a liking for something he, in his superior enlightenment, would think she oughtn't to like; to pass by something at which the truly initiated mind would arrest itself.

Isabel is clearly out of her depth in this company; but not because they are in any true sense deeper than she is. In James's novels, characters who are wealthier and possess a better pedigree often use that "advantage" to browbeat other, "lesser" characters, especially if they are American. Gilbert Osmond has none of these things, but he uses the fact that he is older, better traveled and more worldly in the conventional sense. Thus, he can make the usually independent Isabel feel ill at ease, in spite of the fact that he is nothing more than a diffident amateur art collector and man of leisure. She remains at a distinct disadvantage in dealing with his suave cynicism, in part because she naively yearns to be "truly initiated." The real grossness, we soon realize, is Osmond's, but Isabel will not be allowed to understand that fact until she has suffered the consequences.

The irony in the following passage lies in the fact that Osmond tells Isabel the truth about himself, even if the truth is only a partial one. But, struggling to be as refined and exquisite in her sensibility as she believes he is, she assumes that he is displaying false modesty.

"Have you never made plans?"

"Yes, I made one years ago, and I'm acting on it to-day."

"It must have been a very pleasant one," Isabel permitted herself to observe.

"It was very simple. It was to be as quiet as possible."

"As quiet?" the girl repeated.

"Not to worry—not to strive or struggle. To resign myself. To be content with little." He spoke these sentences slowly, with short pauses between, and his intelligent regard was fixed on his visitor's with the conscious air of a man who has brought himself to confess something.

"Do you call that simple?" she asked with mild irony.

"Yes, because it's negative."

"Has your life been negative?"

"Call it affirmative if you like. Only it has affirmed my indifference. Mind you, not my natural indifference— I *had* none. But my studied, my willful renunciation."

She scarcely understood him; it seemed a question whether he were joking or not. Why should a man who struck her as having a great fund of reserve suddenly bring himself to be so confidential? This was his affair, however, and his confidences were interesting. "I don't see why you should have renounced," she said in a moment.

"Because I could do nothing. I had no prospects, I was poor, and I was not a man of genius. I had no talents even; I took my measure early in life. I was simply the most fastidious gentleman living."

. . . This would have been a rather dry account of Mr. Osmond's career if Isabel had fully believed it; but her imagination supplied the human element which she was sure had not been wanting. His life had been mingled with other lives more than he admitted; naturally she couldn't expect him to enter into this.

Everything about Osmond, to the reader's eye, is studied, suspicious, mildly disreputable: the dramatic slowness with which he speaks, his look, the carefully concocted "confidences" he doles out to Isabel with a doleful gaze. The narrative voice allows us to see things as she does, charitably, and at the same time, to appreciate how she is being taken in, even though we aren't yet sure what Osmond's exact plans are. What we feel is a vague inkling, a desire to take Isabel aside into the next drawing room and warn her to be careful around this man whose manners appear too smooth for comfort.

This inkling is not accidental. Indeed, it has been induced by the use of the narrative voice and point of view. What astounds us is that Isabel does in fact understand the truth about Osmond at the very outset, but her mind rejects that knowledge. "This would have been a rather dry account of Mr. Osmond's career if Isabel had fully believed it; but her imagination supplied the human element which she was sure had not been wanting." His words betray how lifeless and parasitic he is, and he confesses almost brazenly to his lack of talent and ambition. But she, because of her own generous mind, fills in the human warmth so conspicuously missing. Ultimately, the "satellite" reflects back on the protagonist and provides a greater understanding of Isabel's chief character flaw. There is never any attempt to enter into Gilbert Osmond's mind, and yet we learn a great deal about him, in spite of Isabel's trusting nature. This point of view gives us all the intensity of dwelling inside a focal character, combined with many of the advantages one might tend to associate with the "omniscient" narrator that was so popular in novels prior to James's time.

The narrative voice in *The Portrait of a Lady* shows just as much finesse in its handling of point of view as Osmond does in his wooing of Isabel. Because of the way the dialogue meshes with the authorial commentary, Osmond is able to seem forthright without actually being so, and to raise our suspicions without actually having done anything wrong. It will come as no real surprise, later in the novel, that what the "little" Osmond contents himself with in life is to control Isabel, to abuse her money, and to dampen her joy in order to feed his own selfish pleasure. Our closeness to the "center of consciousness" allows

us—or rather, nearly forces us—to share Isabel's intuitive discomfort about Osmond's sudden lack of reserve and his abrupt
confidences. Yet we're kept just separate enough from Isabel
that we cannot come to the same conclusion she does about
"the human element" she believes must reside there inside
him somewhere.

This use of the center of consciousness splits the difference
between taking something at face value and distrusting it completely. By the novel's end, it would be hard to make a case for
the virtues of the devious Osmond. And yet, as far as technique
goes, one could indeed put him forth as a model to be emu-
lated. We should all, as writers, be so successfully manipulative
of our listeners as he is. When it comes down to it, writers all
play a confidence game—our voices smooth, our manners refined, our intentions dishonorable.

FIRST-PERSON NARRATORS AND CHARACTER SYMPATHY

Henry James's novels and stories make a strong argument for
the virtues of the center of consciousness. However, as I have
stated, no point of view is inherently better or worse than another. Rather, they offer different advantages. First-person narrators are capable of establishing character sympathy in a much
more direct and unmediated way. The trade-off is that it is more
demanding to sustain that sympathy for long stretches, because
the writer depends to a greater degree on the particular quality
of the character voice. It affords less room for leverage
"around" the voice. Also, its connection to its "satellites" is
apt to be less direct.

With the use of the first person, the point of view character
(who often doubles as the story or the novel's protagonist),
ends up performing double duty as character and as narrator.
There is no "going outside oneself" in the manner permitted
by Henry James, and therefore the credibility of the narrating
voice is much more likely to fall under suspicion. The narrator
invites us, in effect, to take it or leave it. We, in turn, are more

likely to ask questions about the character's available register of language, whether she would be capable of knowing or saying what is presented on the page as her thoughts and words. Is the diction inconsistent? Does the character's intelligence seem to rise and fall willy-nilly with every minute change in the air, like a cheap thermometer attached to a kitchen window? Third-person narrators tend to offer more range and elicit fewer questions, while first-person narrators, even when they're volatile, offer the advantage of a more immediate and tangible voice.

Some skilled and practiced writers manage to have it both ways, using first-person narrators not restricted to a narrow range of thoughts. Better to risk inconsistency than banish your character-narrator to the land of angst and catatonia. Many of the followers of the style of Raymond Carver or Ann Beattie seem to believe that a first-person narrator requires the speaking voice to be ill-educated, slow-witted or inarticulate. While both of these writers have produced striking effects at times with their adherence to sparc, impoverished language, there is much more to learn from those authors who have respected the intelligence of their creations.

Grace Paley, in *Enormous Changes at the Last Minute,* tends to favor working-class characters in ethnic urban neighborhood settings. But she refuses to pander to the stereotypes about the scope of what these characters might plausibly think or feel. Because of her canny use of narrative voice, the most mundane situations can give way to sudden flights of fancy or speculation that somehow don't seem at all out of keeping with the humble, sometimes poverty-stricken surroundings. One of Paley's most enduring and endearing creations is Faith, a sort of alter ego who constantly finds herself in a state of bemusement and bewilderment about the world she lives in. Faith is streetwise but not cynical, sometimes acerbic and sometimes warm. In the short story, "Wants," the voice sounds wistful about the passage of time, and the mistakes made in the course of a lifetime, but without turning saccharine or succumbing to sheer self-indulgent nostalgia.

> I saw my ex-husband in the street. I was sitting on the
> steps of the new library.
> Hello, my life, I said. We had once been married for
> twenty-seven years, so I felt justified.
> He said What? What life? No life of mine.
> I said, O.K., I don't argue when there's real disagree-
> ment. I got up and went into the library to see how much
> I owed them.
> The librarian said $32 even and you've owed it for
> eighteen years. I didn't deny anything. Because I don't
> understand how time passes. I have had those books. I
> have often thought of them. The library is only two blocks
> away.

One of Paley's methods is deadpan humor and comic under-
statement: "We had once been married for twenty-seven years,
so I felt justified." In this vignette, the narrator succeeds by
being self-effacing. I spent almost my entire adult life with this
man, so I guess I'm entitled to speak to him in a familiar way
on the street—or am I? If we are taken with the voice, we accept
the slightly trumped-up quality of the scene. The conceit asks
one to take for granted the casual encounter on the street after
an unspecified number of years, which quickly gives way to a
conversation, half philosophizing and half warmed-over domestic quarrel. There is little event to be had here, because the
emphasis remains on people standing around talking. Paley's
stories are, more than anything, guided conversations.

Wisely, Paley doesn't allow the urban drawl to go on for
too long, lest it begin to seem like chatter. What strikes us as
wry in brief can begin to seem coy at length. In the story's
mere four pages, this type of narrator is allowed a great deal of
freedom and still engages one's sympathies.

> I wanted to have been married forever to one person,
> my ex-husband or my present one. Either has enough
> character for a whole life, which as it turns out is really
> not such a long time. You couldn't exhaust either man's
> qualities or get under the rock of his reasons in one
> short life.

These ruminations are well-turned, bitter to the heart but pleasing to the ear, and thereby hold our attention. Faith serves as a low-key yet thoughtful docent of the emotions, mainly her own, there on display. These quirks of character hold a certain fascination, like a couple having a half-audible fight in the next booth over. In some of Paley's longer stories, however, the prose begins to meander, and the story's shape begins to give out. The first-person narrative voice, to which most writers gravitate almost instinctively in the beginning, is as full of hazards as the third person—perhaps even fuller.

SIR, I EXIST

One author who has done well in sustaining an idiosyncratic yet appealing first-person narrator at novel length is Walker Percy. What sets Percy's writing apart from most writers is the absolute precision of his social and character observations, and the subtlety with which he uses irony. Even when he makes wickedly sharp observations about human foibles, he seems to cherish others' imperfections as his own. Reading his fiction reminds me of a verse by Stephen Crane, which goes like this: "A man said to the universe:/'Sir, I exist!'/'However,' replied the universe,/'The fact has not created in me/A sense of obligation.' "

In his most celebrated novel, *The Moviegoer*, Percy's description of his protagonist, Binx, falling in love with his secretary, Sharon Kincaid, is masterful in its attention to the concrete details of experience. Binx Bolling, a laissez-faire stockbroker in New Orleans with a penchant for falling for his secretaries, has developed a yen for his latest. As he half listens to his cousin Kate on the telephone, his mind keeps wandering to appreciative thoughts of Sharon.

Sharon seems to pay no attention to these alexandrine conversations, even though we occupy the same small office and she is close enough to touch. Today she wears a sleeveless dress of yellow cotton; her arms come out of the armholes as tenderly as a little girl's. But when she puts her hand to her hair, you can see that it is quite an arm. The soft round muscle goes slack of its own weight. Once she slapped a fly with her bare hand and set my Artmetal desk ringing like a gong. . . . As she types, the little kidney-shaped cushion presses against the small of her back in a nice balance of thrusts.

Percy's use of Binx as narrator keeps this scene from becoming the typical hack treatment of a businessman gazing lecherously at his secretary. To begin with, the voice is genuinely appreciative of the aesthetic value of the moment. Lust may be on the periphery, but still in abeyance. Also, Percy supplies an easygoing humor in Binx's realization of the physical force of Sharon's arm, which contrasts starkly with his initial observation that her arms come out of the dress's armholes "as tenderly as a little girl's." These details, apart from their momentary descriptive value, do significant work in setting the reader up for the unfolding of their relationship.

For, as it turns out, Sharon is anything but "a little girl." The muscle that goes slack of its own weight will be reflected later in the novel when it turns out that Sharon has by far the upper hand in the relationship between the two. Binx hasn't yet cottoned to the fact that he will soon be the fly on the Artmetal desk. This first-person voice, because it is allowed sufficient self-awareness, performs characterization and plot development in subtle ways, even as it charms and entertains us with its attentiveness to the moment. Binx's voice becomes, by turns, giddy, courtly, satirical and tender. These rapid changes of tone remain especially possible with the kind of intimate, yet comic and quietly sardonic, narrator used by Percy. These changes of tone would, however, be more difficult to achieve in third-person narration.

I am in love with Sharon Kincaid. She knows nothing of this, I think. I have not asked her for a date nor even been specially friendly. On the contrary: I have been aloof and correct as a Nazi officer in occupied Paris. Yet when she came in this morning unshouldering her Guatemalan bag and clearing her hair from her short collar, I heard a soughing sound in my ears like a desert wind. The Guatemalan bag contains *Peyton Place*, I happen to know. . . . My Sharon should not read this kind of stuff.

Her person has acquired a priceless value to me. For the first time, I understand the conceits of the old poets: how I envy thee, little kidney-shaped cushion! Oh, to take thy place and press in thy stead against the sweet hollow of her back, etc. . . .

Toward her, I keep a Gregory Peckish sort of distance. I am a tall black-headed fellow and I know as well as he how to keep to myself, make my eyes fine and my cheeks spare, tuck my lip and say a word or two with a nod or two.

Binx, with his usual cool irony, is lovesick, or at least hopelessly infatuated, but at the same time acutely aware of the absurdity of his and Sharon's mutual pretenses as they strike the poses required by the rules of their professional relationship. When in doubt, he acts the way he thinks Gregory Peck would in a similar situation. The effect of the passage comes from the razor-sharp accuracy of his eye for characterization, without which the more "sociological" aspect of his satire wouldn't be convincing.

THE UNRELIABLE NARRATOR AND CHARACTER VOICE

Sympathy, however, isn't the only response that fiction writers want to evoke in their readers. Some of the most memorable characters in modern fiction are ones on whom bestowing approval or withholding it is beside the point. Using an unreliable narrator can make available kinds of characters that you might normally shy away from. It opens up a broader range of humanity. The way that you employ voice with an unreliable narrator lets you give that character full range in speaking his mind. The voice can be as opinionated, amoral, ruthless, petty, etc., as you like, while the unreliability built into the point of view subtly invites the reader not to take what is being said at face value. In the meantime, you persuade your reader to broaden himself by inhabiting sometimes extreme perspectives, seeing how he feels from the inside.

In Albert Camus's *The Stranger,* the convicted murderer Meursault is a compelling amoral figure, one who neither asks nor expects to be "liked." He is much more interested in understanding his condition in the cosmos than in copping a plea for himself. Camus makes a deliberate choice at the novel's beginning to work with an unreliable first-person narrator, one sure to keep us on edge. The relentless probing into the fundamental nature of existence undertaken in *The Stranger* requires a certain edginess. Meursault, to be sure, is no Huck Finn.

> Mother died today. Or, maybe yesterday; I can't be sure. The telegram from the Home says: YOUR MOTHER PASSED AWAY. FUNERAL TOMORROW. DEEP SYMPA-THY. Which leaves the matter doubtful; it could have been yesterday.

This uncertainty as to the time of the telegram's arrival, in the novel's very first paragraph, initiates the tone of disorientation that prevails throughout *The Stranger,* set in the scorching heat of Algeria. Camus is smart; he raises lack of certainty from a mere point of view to a virtual state. Establishing this sense of the unreliability of Meursault's narrative account early on is important, since he is to be put on trial later in the course of events. What remains in question is not whether Meursault has killed a man, but what has led him to do it. The frustrated search for the answer to that question is the stuff of enduring fiction.

In the company of his friend Raymond, who is being more or less pursued by a pair of faceless Arabs in blue dungarees who have some sort of grudge against him, Meursault goes along for the ride. At the moment of the murder, Camus bears down on the sensation of the fundamental inexplicability, not only of events, but of human nature and human motives. For

Camus, the use of an unreliable narrator is not simply a convenient device, but an organic expression of the themes that drive the story.

> The sound of the waves was even lazier, feebler, than at noon. But the light hadn't changed; it was pounding as fiercely as ever on the long stretch of sand that ended at the rock. For two hours the sun seemed to have made no progress; becalmed in a sea of molten steel. Far out on the horizon a steamer was passing; I could just make out from the corner of my eye the small black moving patch, while I kept my gaze fixed on the Arab.
> It struck me that all I had to do was to turn, walk away, and think no more about it. But the whole beach, pulsing with heat, was pressing on my back. I took some steps toward the stream. The Arab didn't move. After all, there was still some distance between us.

The next thing he knows, Meursault has taken a fateful and fatal step forward, the Arab's knife flashes and Meursault shoots him. There is no passion involved in the encounter, nor any motive. What remains significant here is the way that Camus sets up the novel so that his first-person point of view character's account is given as the "testimony" of a defendant, and yet we are encouraged to doubt the veracity and reliability of his account—not because he is deliberately lying, but because the drowsy, but hallucinatory and relentless heat of Algeria clouds his head, and by extension, clouds ours.

Because of the use of the first person, the sensory details of the beach scene stand out as not only exceedingly clear, but subjectively distorted to reflect Meursault's state of mind. We stand as close to him as we can possibly get in the moments before the killing takes place. We should know full well what happens, and why. We hear the sound of the waves, and watch and feel the sun as a mass of molten steel suspended over the water. Every aspect of the scene appears calm, lazy, better conducive to a nap than to a murder. That is why it is all the more maddening that, in spite of the narrator's professing "all I had to do was to turn, walk away, and think no more about it," he goes ahead and commits the violent act. In terms of narative perspective, we're right on top of him, like a cheap summer suit on a beachcomber, and yet we're made to feel that we've missed something crucial.

That feeling is provoked by the way the description is guided by the unreliable narrator. He obstinately refuses to answer the question "Why?" The only explanation given is a sensory one, as befits the desultory but also hallucinatory voice of this hemmed-in narrator. "But the whole beach, pulsing with heat, was pressing on my back." This lapidary explanation represents the feeblest of all defenses, and yet, from our vantage point, under the rays of the sun and within earshot of the beach, it is a persuasive defense. One need not "like" Meursault to be brought over to his vision of events.

It has often been said that the "unreliable" narrator is one whom a reader instinctively distrusts, but it becomes clear, in the case of *The Stranger,* that to distrust and to dislike are not at all the same thing. For a fiction writer, the advantage of employing an unreliable narrator is to keep the reader off balance in strategic ways, so that character motives can be entered into more deeply and more unexpectedly. Too much sympathy can preclude a thorough inspection of human perversity. In terms of technique, Camus, unlike James, is not the least bit interested in supplying himself with the extra leverage that comes with the use of a center of consciousness.

After the authorities take Meursault into custody and interrogate him, they place him in a jail cell with barely enough room to turn around in. "Some days later I was put by myself in a cell, where I slept on a plank bed attached to the wall. The only other furniture was a latrine bucket and a tin basin." That is precisely how Camus would like his reader to feel, that there is no breathing room, let alone a drawing room to take aside the protagonist and explain things to him, no way to fully detach oneself from the inexorable flow of unpleasant sensation. This narrative instead drives us onward, staggering, without much in the way of authorial commentary, like a prisoner being hurried along by a brusque and silent guard.

Only later, during the trial, does Camus allow the novel's

central ideas to display themselves. But even those sequences are mildly hallucinatory, and by that point in the novel, everything exists only in retrospect, introduced as evidence, which again puts the reader in the position of having to pass moral judgment on prior actions, a member of the jury. In this way, Camus uses voice and point of view to remain true to his novel's aims.

SWITCHING POINT OF VIEW

Sometimes you need to experiment with different narrative points of view and different qualities of character voice to be sure you have found the one most suitable and most advantageous to your purposes. I've frequently made this suggestion to my creative writing students. For instance, one woman wrote a story based on her grandmother and titled it "A Mind Apart." Like many beginning writers, she had opted for the first-person point of view, falsely believing it would instantly lend the sense of immediacy she was after.

The effect she produced was quite the opposite, and it wasn't until she tried a third-person narrator, the supposedly more "distant" one, that she created the momentum she wanted. In my initial comment to her, I urged her to rethink the point of view she had chosen. To do so, I had to link this issue firmly to the question of voice. Changing point of view implies a change in tone and language, if it is not to be merely a mechanical shift. The connection between voice and point of view can have profound consequences for the story as a whole, including its plot and structure. To help the student understand this connection, I suggested she read Katherine Anne Porter's "The Jilting of Granny Weatherall." Porter uses a third-person narration while giving it all the immediacy and verve that we most readily associate with first person. Because Porter understands keenly the substantial effect of voice on point of view, she can employ a modified "stream of consciousness" that manages to seem both inside and outside Granny

Weatherall. The resulting prose is a combination of elegance and urgency, tautness and tortuousness.

The story begins with a direct sentence, innocuous enough: "She flicked her wrist neatly out of Doctor Harry's pudgy careful fingers and pulled the sheet up to her chin." Before long, this mild gesture of defiance gives way to an intense inner dialogue, as Granny reviews her life and remembers how she held up under its overbearing demands, in spite of being jilted by her lover at the altar and then later having lost her "second" husband.

> It had been a hard pull, but not too much for her. When she thought of all the food she had cooked, and all the clothes she had cut and sewed, and all the gardens she had made—well, the children showed it. There they were, made out of her, and they couldn't get away from that. Sometimes she wanted to see John again and point to them and say, Well I didn't do so badly, did I? . . . She used to think of him as a man, but now all the children were older than their father, and he would be a child beside her if she saw him now. It seemed strange and there was something wrong in the idea. Why, he couldn't possibly recognize her. She had fenced in a hundred acres once, digging the post holes herself and clamping the wires with just a negro boy to help. That changed a woman. John would be looking for a young woman with the peaked Spanish comb in her hair and the painted fan. Digging post holes changed a woman.

And voice, like digging post holes, also changes a woman. Porter preserves, even on Granny's deathbed, especially there, all of the woman's energy, rage and vital force. Though the last words of the story are "She stretched herself with a deep breath and blew out the light," signalling Granny Weatherall's death, she nonetheless rages against the dying of the light. With her body all but expired, sheer voice keeps her alive in those final delirious, poignant hours. The almost imperceptibly distanced third-person point of view, on the other hand, tempers this rage and our understanding of it. It keeps us at a slight remove, like the gentle restraint of the undertaker who keeps the distraught spouse from leaping into the open grave of the deceased.

Be bold in experimenting with point of view. If you feel dissatisfied with a story, in spite of your fascination with its subject and characters, try changing the point of view. It will genuinely make you see the story through a different pair of eyes. And don't feel that you have to choose as narrators only those kinds of characters close to your experience. What's so appealing about the different narrative perspectives available to you is that they allow you to split the difference between how you, as a human being, tend to see things and how you, as a writer, dare to imagine them.

Exercises

1. Write a two-page sketch in which you employ a third-person "center of consciousness." Your emphasis should be on exploiting and exploring the character's blind spots, and the gaps between what the character knows and what those around him know. As James often does, you might want to begin by working with a character who is something of an ingenue. Remember that although the point of view is not first person, it still expresses the focal character's thoughts and feelings.

2. Concoct a three-page vignette in the manner of Paley or Percy in which your main object is to create a sympathetic first-person character voice. Allow the character to digress as much as you wish, but try to maintain a consistency of mood.

3. Write a story in which the narrator is unreliable. The narrator does not have to be lying, but rather should have less than a total grasp of the consequences of what is going on around him or her. At the same time, this character should be able to describe the specifics of the events in sharp detail.

CHAPTER 3

ATMOSPHERE
AND TONE

I WAS GIVING A WRITING LESSON to a friend of mine, sitting at her dining room table in an apartment that seemed to have windows in every whitewashed wall of every room to let in light. After a long winter, the weather had turned, the tulips had opened a few tentative petals to test whether the sudden flood of sunshine was a trick, and my friend had shoved up the heavy windows stuck fast to the sash for many months. The release made them groan with pleasure, like someone whose lungs can finally breathe after a long season of chills and catarrh. Each of us had places to be later, but my friend Celeste and I were in about as much of a hurry as cats on a warm sill, and she doodled in her notebook.

Celeste is a lithe six-footer with Irish hair and the freckles to go with it. A former basketball jock who tends toward the esoteric, she's fast on the court but takes her sweet time elsewhere in life. "Guy Smiley," she said, for that's what she usually calls me, "get to the point." But the point appeared, precisely, to not be too hasty about anything on such a day, when the glow of the hardwood floor made the little apartment expand out in all directions, gradually melting into the larger world outside, like a trompe l'oeil diorama, where you can't tell where the painting leaves off and the figures begin.

"Did your landlord just paint those walls?"

Celeste took a long drink from her glass of clorophyll water, jade green. She herself is a long drink of water. "Nah. But he's on an improvement jag. They refinished the floors a couple of weeks ago. His maintenance people never stop. Perpetual motion.''

"Mm," I replied.

With the windows open, we could hear bits of the indolent chat of the Southside workers who were supposed to be laying a new concrete sidewalk outside. "Over dere," the foreman sighed. "It needs to go flush with the other one."

"I don't know. I don't t'ink so," another offered. But the subaltern wasn't really objecting. In fact, I had the feeling that they weren't actually working, and had instead stretched out under one of the blossoming dogwoods in their spackled caps to smoke cigarettes and cop a little midday shade. Their conversation only existed in the realm of the hypothetical. They weren't about to lay any more slabs until the sun passed behind a cloud.

My mind became distracted by the fluttering of the lace curtains next to the open window a few feet away. Celeste keeps lace curtains in all her windows. Patches of sunlight fell in long bands across the opposite end of the room. The air stirred, lifting and lilting the curtains, and made me feel as if I, too, were sprawled somewhere beneath leafy branches. Why was it that the translucent curtains made the air feel cooler and more caressing to me, when my mind was sure that they didn't have any real scientific effect on the temperature of the breeze?

"I don't know," I said, even though Celeste hadn't asked me a question.

Atmosphere can be defined as a physical setting enlivened by mood. We tend to associate moods with people, as when someone says "Best not talk to her. She's in a bad mood today." But when mood is ascribed to a place, it becomes atmosphere. Keep in mind, however, that in fiction, a setting is almost always populated by characters, and understood through them. The mood, then, belongs to characters and setting simultaneously. Together, they create the atmosphere. In the above example, one can say that Celeste and I are in a lazy, carefree mood because of the weather, the open windows, the time of day. Or, conversely, one could say that in fiction, the elements are conditioned by our mindset, so that we end up deciding that it's a "lazy day." In a sense, it doesn't make much difference which comes first, because both "moods" have to work together to create the atmosphere.

CREATING A PRIVATE LANDSCAPE

Eudora Welty, in the opening of *Delta Wedding*, uses a spring breeze of her own, though for other purposes. With an identical detail to the one I used above, she is able to create a quite different effect, one of anticipation and movement rather than lassitude. As she describes the journey through the Mississippi Delta by Laura McRaven on the train the Yellow Dog, the cadences of Welty's prose mimic the carefree movement of the train and its passengers.

> In the passenger car every window was propped open with a stick of kindling wood. A breeze blew through, hot and then cool, fragrant of the woods and yellow flowers and of the train. The yellow butterflies flew in at any window, out at any other, and outdoors one of them could keep up with the train, which then seemed to be racing with a butterfly.

Creating atmosphere is not simply a matter of sticking in the right details, such as a warm breeze to indicate spring. Atmosphere is of little interest to the fiction writer in the sense that the weather forecaster might use that word, in conjunction with high pressure systems and cold fronts and a national map with curving arrows pointing this way and that, pretending to be able to predict something that is, by its very essence, capricious.

Being able to communicate the natural and man-made world in a tactile way is certainly part of what makes Welty's prose delicious, but if the intent were only to dazzle us with the sumptuousness of springtime in the Deep South, then the description would qualify as merely decorative, and one would have to call the effect atmospherics rather than atmosphere. And the difference between atmospherics and atmosphere is approximately the difference between theatrics and theater. Theatrics is histrionic, hysterical, added-on emotion. Theater, on the other hand, is acting that comes from a genuine engagement with the text of the play. Likewise, atmosphere, though it comes from the wellspring of character emotion, finds its objective expression in the setting.

Instead of description for its own sake, Welty means to convey Laura's state of mind as she approaches the homeplace of her cousins, the Fairchilds, for purposes of attending a wedding. Her mind is so overpowered by the beginnings of this new experience that she can process it at this point in her journey only in terms of her senses, and not her intelligence. The image of the butterfly outside the window underscores the peculiar feeling of being in a train, with its unique combination of motion and stillness. Laura is, as T.S. Eliot would put it, "the still point of the turning world."

How is it that butterflies can fly casually and at will in and out of the windows of a moving train? How can a butterfly even keep pace with a train, much less squander excess motion making careless loops in the air? These acts seem to run counter to the laws of physics, and yet they are happening, as easily as you please. Best, then, not to think too hard about it, and just experience the pure sensation. In Welty's confident handling of atmosphere, Laura becomes, in short order, the human equivalent of the butterfly, a delicate yet strangely sturdy creature borne aloft on the wind.

> Thoughts went out of her head and the landscape filled it. In the Delta, most of the world seemed sky. The clouds were large—larger than the horses or houses, larger than boats or churches or gins, larger than anything except the fields the Fairchilds planted.

She is dwarfed by her surroundings, buffeted by them, but wisely, she doesn't resist. Gradually, human concerns overtake sheer landscape, for ultimately, it is Laura's relation to the boisterous and loving Delta clan, and not the scenery of the Yazoo River, that makes for the novel's central interest. The atmosphere exists for her sake rather than she for its sake. The laws of fiction, not the laws of physics, prevail. The contradictory sensations of stillness and motion, of pleasant disorientation that gets established on the first page, continue as she is swept into the enveloping hubbub of the cousins who have come to greet her.

> Through the windows Laura could see five or six cousins at once, all jumping up and down at different moments. Each mane of light hair waved like a holiday banner. . . . When Mr. Terry set her on the little iron steps . . . and gave her a spank, she staggered, and was lifted down among flying arms to the earth. . . . She was kissed and laughed at and her hat would have been snatched away but for the new elastic that pulled it back, and then she was half-carried along like a drunken reveler at a festival, not quite recognizing who anyone was.

No particular landscape or set of images is endowed with a singular, particular meaning. A writer bestows on private images a more public meaning. A reader does not want to be given a cliché equating flowers with love, or crosses with holiness, or dead leaves with aging. In that case, the fiction writer simply borrows from a stockpile of ready-made images, without adding to them the energy of her inner life. The assocations we develop with the objects in our world are just as idiosyncratic and intimate as those feelings we have about people meaningful to us. On the other hand, if the language offered is too private, it will be indecipherable. The challenge is to keep up the intensity of private associations while sharing their secret meanings through prose.

EVERY MAN HIS OWN SALAMANDER

I, for instance, have a particular feeling about an unusual type of lizard known as an axolotl, because my first encounter with one happened at the time when I was falling in love with the woman I would eventually marry. She worked in a molecular biology lab at the university we both attended as undergraduates, and one autumn night, while we were out walking together through campus, she offered to show me the collection of axolotls housed in the biology building. The collection had a reputation as the largest of its kind, and she said that the miniscule beasts continued to exist more or less in their prehistoric state.

The cavernous building was empty and somewhat decrepit, the edges of the marble steps worn, the glass of the display cases yellowed, the steam radiators banging and cracking, the atmosphere unseasonably swampy, the brothy smell of agar reeking from the petri dishes—the way that science buildings get, in short. With the lights in the hallways turned off, leaving only the flickering neon glow of the glass cases with their superannuated science displays, I suppose that the encounter with these beings from a primordial yesteryear could have seemed creepy, even sinister. All the novelistic possibilities for such a treatment hovered there in abundance.

But I was flushed with love, and had been necking with my girlfriend in the woods outside Jordan Hall, and I had worked myself into that state of giddiness that people who aren't in love find highly annoying. Therefore, the near-transparency of the axolotls in their terrariums seemed to reflect only too well the open, trusting, even naive transparency of my own heart. I was a Visible Man, the kind whose guts can be perused on the display shelf of better toy stores by budding scientists, and I had nothing to hide. I was also being initiated into the world of my beloved, a world whose mystery was embodied in the silent and grotesque beauty of the axolotls. At that moment, I would have been willing to take one home to my dorm room and keep it as a pet. Their translucent bodies seemed no more threatening to me than the Gummi Bears I now buy for my daughter out of the glass jar atop the counter of our local delicatessen.

I might have eventually ended up writing a story about that encounter between man and beast, except that at the very same time, I had been reading a book of short stories by Julio Cortázar, and the one that had made the greatest impression on

me was called, coincidentally enough, "Axolotl." The famous
Argentine had beat me to the punch by a couple of decades,
and the complex of associations concerning his axolotls, much
darker than the ones in my benevolent world, compelled and
fascinated me, made a spectator of me, and the power of
his atmosphere made me suspend my own shimmering image
of the salamander so that I could, instead, participate in
Cortázar's narrator's tale of an obsessive and destructive
prehistoric cosmos.

> There was a time when I thought a great deal about
> the axolotls. I went to see them in the aquarium at the
> Jardin des Plantes and stayed for hours watching them,
> observing their immobility, their faint movements. Now I
> am an axolotl.

Here, one begins to enter into the complement to atmosphere
that goes by the name of *tone.* One speaks of tones in music
and color, and perhaps the fictional term is borrowed from
those sister arts, but tone has a special meaning for fiction writers. Tone has everything to do with who is telling the story, but
it should not be confused with point of view. In the simplest
sense, one may begin to define tone in the manner one uses it
when saying that so-and-so spoke in a certain "tone of voice."
That voice might be pleased, fearful, irritated, etc. But the tonal
qualities of a passage of prose fiction are, ideally, much more
nuanced. A succinct definition of tone would be the dispersal
of the narrative voice into every word of the story. This act of
dispersal makes tone difficult to locate. It is an attitude toward
the events being told, but this attitude does not reside in any
single character, not even the point-of-view character, since it
is also intermingled with authorial attitude.

In the above passage, Cortázar deliberately begins by being
as straightforward as possible. In this first-person narration,
there are no murky or lugubrious atmospherics to prepare the
way for the rather startling announcement made at the end
of the story's first paragraph. Instead, we are given only basic
information about the aquarium's location, after which the nar-

rator says, "Now I am an axolotl." The authorial tone of voice says to us, in effect, "I want you to believe and accept, for the purposes of this story, at least as a speculative proposition, that a human being literally turned into an axolotl."

WRITING THE LIGHT FANTASTIC

This authorial decision to eliminate the kind of traditional suspense that marks gothic horror stories opens us instead to the psychological uncertainties of being. Cortázar has no interest in plot as an end in itself, in making us feel that something "unbelievable" has happened, or in telling us an "incredible" story. Quite the opposite is true. If Cortázar had wanted to gussy up the ghoulish rhetoric and milk the atmosphere for its own sake, then he would have saved the "revelation" of the man's "horrible" condition for the end of the story, instead of revealing it at the beginning in an almost offhand way. As it is, he presents the transformation as perhaps not an everyday occurrence, but certainly as something that could happen to anyone on any given day, given the right combination of circumstances. We are asked to accept, as a momentary idea, that the unthinkable, even the impossible, could happen to someone like us.

In criticizing another practitioner of the mode, Cortázar makes clear his own way of approaching the material.

The fantastic stories of H.P. Lovecraft don't interest me in the slightest because the fantasy element strikes me as completely fabricated and artificial. Everything takes place in old houses, with wind howling in the dining room, and once he's managed to terrify the ingenuous reader, he lets loose a few hairy beasts and curses from mysterious gods, which was okay a couple of centuries ago, when that sort of thing made everybody shiver, but which actually, at least for me, lacks all interest. Fantasy is something very simple, something that could happen in broad daylight, at high noon, right now between you and me, or on the subway, while you were on your way to this encounter.

I agree it's something exceptional, but there's no reason it has to differentiate itself from the manifestations of this reality that surrounds us. Fantasy happens without any spectacular modification of things. For me, the fantastic is simply a sudden indication that, at the borders of Aristotle's laws, and of our reasoning mind, perfectly valid mechanisms exist, right now, that our logical mind can't fathom but that at certain moments erupt and make themselves felt.

In "Axolotl," this mundane eruption of the fantastic requires that the tone of the first-person narrator be obsessive, but at the same time meticulous, even scientific, in its descriptions.

> In the library . . . I consulted a dictionary and learned that axolotls are the larval stage (provided with gills) of a species of salamander of the genus Ambystoma. That they were Mexican I knew already by looking at them and their little pink Aztec faces and the placard at the top of the tank.

We're given the option of believing that he is a madman, completely self-deluded, or that, on the contrary, he is an essentially normal person who is just describing the monumental metamorphosis that overtook him in the course of an otherwise uneventful life.

> Inexpressive features, with no other trait save the eyes, two orifices, like brooches, wholly of transparent gold, lacking any life but looking, letting themselves be penetrated by my look, which seemed to travel past the golden level and lose itself in a diaphanous interior mystery.

The atmosphere, in this case, follows from the tone of the description. Instead of supplying us straight off with "old houses, with wind howling in the dining room," Cortázar uses the narrator's relentless description to gradually create a mood that pervades the tale and creates a progressive sense of claustrophobia. Again, it's the dispersal of the narrative voice into every word of the story—a technique, for sure, but not a ploy.

And what exactly does this tone consist of in "Axolotl"? It wouldn't be accurate to describe this character as overwrought, like the man in Edgar Allan Poe's "The Tell-Tale Heart," who can scarcely contain himself from confessing his crime of killing the man with the vulture eye and nailing him beneath the floorboards of his room. Nonetheless, there is a tense quality to Cortázar's narrator's tale, as he tries to convey his simultaneous emotions of rapture and fear. He insists on drawing attention to the axolotls' proto-human features, while at the same time suggesting there exists within them a secret intelligence, something pre-Columbian or even more ancient, something that has to do with fathomless depths of time.

This is remarkable, considering the scale of the creatures. Part of Cortázar's skill lies in his ability to create a tempest in a teapot. Note that the "landscape" by no means strikes one as all-encompassing or grand, as in Welty's novel, where the clouds seem to envelop Laura in their hugeness. Here, just the inverse is true. The man's gaze fastens onto a microcosmic world, no larger than a zoo terrarium. The effect would be different, and much milder, if he had chosen to literally deposit his protagonist in some enormous prehistoric jungle, running from gargantuan and thunderous monsters or dinosaurs, as often happens in Saturday morning B movies.

What disturbs is that the literal atmosphere is so small and tame, and yet the narrator, through the tone of his language, invests the terrain and its miniscule inhabitants with a sinister depth capable of swallowing the man into their malevolence. How can he be overtaken by such an insignificant thing? And yet, the language of "Axolotl"—its tone, and the atmosphere created by that tone—persuades us that the transformation is not only possible, but inevitable.

Cortázar's sleight of hand intensifies when he has the narrator begin to slip in allusions to the "present" moment of the story, and we are reminded that the "man" is telling us his tale from inside the terrarium glass—thus, he has already become an axolotl by the time the story begins.

> It's that we don't enjoy moving a lot, and the tank is
> so cramped—we barely move in any direction and we're
> hitting one of the others with our tail or our head—diffi-
> culties arise, fights, tiredness. The time feels like it's less if
> we stay quietly.

Cortázar is able to create an atmosphere of asphyxiation, of
walls closing in, by the simple act of beginning to alternate
between referring to the axolotls as "we" and "they." Here,
point of view is really an outgrowth of tone rather than vice
versa. Most often, tone follows from point of view, but in this
case, Cortázar seems to have settled first on a certain quality of
language, and then proceeded to give it a human face—or
rather, an animal one.

Precisely by not insisting on this point too hard at the beginning, and by not trying to force on us a laborious and over-
heated "atmosphere" throughout, he is able to convey, at the
story's end, the true sense of nightmare-as-reality, as the truth
dawns on the narrator about his transformed condition.

> To realize that was, for the first moment, like a man
> buried alive awakening to his fate. . . . The horror began—
> I learned in the same moment—of believing myself pris-
> oner in the body of an axolotl, metamorphosed into him
> with my human mind intact buried alive in an axolotl,
> condemned to move lucidly among unconscious crea-
> tures.

This idea of moving lucidly among unconscious creatures, or
conversely, of moving unconsciously among lucid creatures,
has been played with in such novels as William Faulkner's *The
Sound and the Fury,* in the section narrated by the idiot Benjy,
in Daniel Keyes's *Flowers for Algernon,* in the diary of a retarded
man who becomes a genius and then progressively loses his
ability to reason again, and in Dalton Trumbo's *Johnny Got His
Gun,* in the account of a quadriplegic ex-soldier whose body is
virtually destroyed while his mind remains perfectly alert and
cogent. The inspiration of Cortázar was to play out this poignant and archetypal human drama in the most insignificant

and "unreasonable" of theaters. To see the world in a grain of sand is an easy enough thing to do, but to get your reader to inhabit that grain of sand requires a subtlety of voice only available through the proper handling of tone.

Always be aware of the crucial relation between your character and his, her or—in Cortázar's case—its setting. Choose your settings based not on their exotic appeal, or because they are part of your homeplace, but on what they help reveal about how your characters think and feel. Just as you speak of a person feeling completely comfortable and confident in a given situation as being "in her element," so you can use setting as an opportunity to reveal aspects of that character not made evident by dialogue and interactions with other characters in the story. Creating atmosphere, or putting a character in her element, will make the setting a virtual extension of character.

METAFICTION AND TONE

I now want to give some attention to metafiction to help illustrate the importance of tone. Because metafiction puts extra demands on the reader, one can see all the more clearly the role tone plays in satisfying a reader's expectation of pleasure. Finding the right tone for telling your story can allow you to get away with things that your reader otherwise wouldn't put up with, at least not for very long. The Czech novelist Milan Kundera is fond of browbeating his readers, but he does it in a charming way so his bullying becomes a pleasure. Often he incorporates into his novels elements of what is called metafiction: fiction that comments on the processes and difficulties of writing fiction. Usually, the traditional elements of story such as plot and character are made more flexible, so that the author can intrude into the story almost at will to comment on anything he sees fit. Often, digressions of various lengths let the author discourse about life and literature, and the puzzling relation between the two.

This "modern" use of metafiction goes back at least to the eighteenth century, to Laurence Sterne's celebrated novel *The*

Life and Opinions of Tristram Shandy, the granddaddy of metafiction and a popular work in its own day. The device has been used with varying degrees of success ever since. In the U.S., fiction writers had a heyday with metafiction in the 1960s, though the intense enthusiasm for this playfulness fairly quickly dried up, and critics began to speak of the tendency as "arid" and "bankrupt." Today, those few fiction writers who try their hand at metafiction and are lucky enough to have their books reviewed, usually find themselves the object of heated criticism on the part of reviewers who are outraged that the author couldn't "just tell the story."

To understand this misguided response, to comprehend why a novelist such as Kundera has been an international success "in spite of" his experimenting, and to be able to have this technique at our disposal, we have to make some subtle distinctions. Why is it that Laurence Sterne's novel is still in print, and seems as fresh today as it did two hundred years ago? To give a satisfactory answer to that question, one ultimately has to come back to the issue of tone.

The trick, if it can be called that, of integrating metafiction into storytelling is to realize that fiction writing is, to some extent, always a process of tinkering with a reader's expectations about the form. You as a writer may decide to satisfy those expectations or not, but whenever you don't meet them, there is the chance of annoying your audience. For someone reading a story that abruptly breaks off time after time, or changes the personality of the characters at will, or makes the authorial voice quarrel with the narrator, the implied question is "What's the payoff for me? What do I get in return for suspending my expectations?"

If the answer doesn't become fairly clear, there isn't much incentive to keep reading. The story begins to seem self-indulgent, perhaps pointless, a juvenile celebration of the author's mastery of "technique." On the other hand, if the metafictional tendencies appear in service of greater human insight, of deepening the story's plumb into existence, of widening its scope, then the increased demand on an intelligent reader may indeed be worth the effort. In the end, the "trick" can't come off as merely tricky. There must be a reason.

Author and Character

The impression the story makes will depend, as I have said, to a large degree on the tone established at the beginning and sustained throughout the performance. This point has been missed by many a writer who has toyed with the form leading to unfortunate consequences. Milan Kundera, however, knows just how far to push, and there is a sense of fun, passion and compassion to his prose that buoys up his philosophical and aesthetic "digressions." Part four of *The Book of Laughter and Forgetting* begins with a lament about the difficulty of authoring characters.

> According to my calculations there are two or three new fictional characters baptized on earth every second. As a result, I am always unsure of myself when it comes time to enter that vast crowd of John the Baptists. But what can I do? I have to call my characters something, don't I? Well, this time, just to make it clear my heroine belongs to me and me alone (and means more to me than anyone ever has), I am giving her a name no woman has ever had before: Tamina. I picture her as tall and beautiful, thirty-three, and a native of Prague.

Kundera invites us to commiserate with him about the old problem of there being nothing new under the sun. "I have to call my characters something, don't I?" His complaint is undertaken in a comic spirit, for of course he hasn't the slightest intention of giving up his writing. He is rather trying to win us over, like the groom at the wedding dinner party, nervous that his old friends, who have traveled long distances for the occasion, won't find his new wife as charming and irresistible as he knows her to be. So, he ends up making a casual disclaimer about her outfit, saying that apparently the tailor didn't get it quite right, and it doesn't suit her figure as well as the things she usually wears. The ploy is so transparent, it's hard not to let oneself be taken in by it.

Prudently, Kundera doesn't allow the business about naming characters to go on for too long. Instead, he changes the subject, but sustains the endearing tone, although now he's gotten his confidence up (like the groom, after a couple more glasses of champagne), and is in a mood to hold forth about the foibles of human character. He is still working in a metafictional vein, but has modulated into another register—pleasantly cocky, one might call it. All the while, he also goes about the business of fleshing out his newly created "beautiful" character, who works as a café waitress.

> Tamina serves the customers their coffee . . . and then goes back to her place behind the bar. There is almost always someone sitting on a bar stool wanting to talk to her. They all like her. She is a good listener.
>
> But does she really listen? Or does she just look on, silent and preoccupied? I can't quite tell, and it really doesn't matter that much. What does matter is that she never interrupts anybody. You know what it's like when two people start a conversation. First one of them does all the talking, the other breaks it off with "That's just like me, I . . ." and goes on talking about himself until his partner finds a chance to say, "That's just like me, I . . ."
>
> . . . All man's life among men is nothing more than a battle for the ears of others. The whole secret of Tamina's popularity is that she has no desire to talk about herself.

A number of things happen simultaneously in this passage, and they are managed above all by tone. First, it becomes clear that in his initial complaint about naming characters, the author/narrator was not simply talking about the process of fiction. Rather, it was his first statement of the theme of humans' illusions about their uniqueness. Everybody wants to be an individual, and so each must insist at all costs that any conversation constantly return to a catalogue of his or her own tastes, preferences, habits: "That's just like me, I . . ." Kundera is able to tweak the reader about this, because he is at the same time critical and indulgent of this human foible. We're more willing to confess to our narcissism if we know that allowances for it are going to be made.

Second, Kundera is quite cagey in getting his pet character characterized. Remember that he began by worrying that Tamina, who "means more to me than anyone ever has," wouldn't stand out in a crowd. Ironically, however, what makes her unique is that she is the only one, according to Kundera, who *doesn't* insist on her uniqueness, who doesn't try to turn the conversation back to herself. This talent for listening in silence allows her to achieve what none of the others seem capable of doing. Her quiet ways qualify her to be one of the novel's protagonists. Thus, Kundera's "digression" does as much work to flesh out his character as could have been accomplished in a traditional scene.

Third, his tone of comic playfulness and mock seriousness allows him to make grand philosophical statements without losing the thread of his novel. "All man's life among men is nothing more than a battle for the ears of others." He can speak at this level of generality because he undercuts his own language, always returning, in the end, to Tamina and her lonely life as a café waitress. This "novel of ideas" is more than anything a personal, even intimate, conversation. Before long, he moves into the heart of a story about Tamina, her diffident sexual liaison with Hugo, and her complicated friendship with Bibi.

Kundera's use of metafiction is his way of laying the groundwork for the unfolding of the plot by periodically taking us into his confidence. In the end, he seems to be saying that no matter what philosphical edifices authors build, characters will stubbornly and perversely refuse to live in them. They go their own way, without giving up any of their idiosyncracies for the sake of a godlike author who wants to pull it all together. Knowing this, Kundera manages his own processes of fiction making and thinking through a tone of self-effacing wit about his own limitations, along with a determination to create, as best he can, flawed characters for whom he feels compassion and interest.

Drawbacks of Pure Metafiction

Compare Kundera's handling of tone to that of John Barth, who is probably the most celebrated metafictionist of our times. Barth is an unquestionably brilliant technician, and he has taken his preferred form to its highest level. Yet even in his early work, such as "Life Story," the first story to earn him his reputation, one can see the drawbacks of working in too narrow or too "pure" of a mode. The subject of "Life Story" is a man trying in vain to write down the story of his life.

> Without discarding what he'd already written he began his story afresh in a somewhat different manner. Whereas his earlier version had opened in a straight-forward documentary fashion and then degenerated or at least modulated intentionally into irrealism and dissonance he decided this time to tell his tale from start to finish in a conservative, "realistic," unself-conscious way. He being by vocation an author of novels and stories it was perhaps inevitable that one afternoon the possibility would occur to the writer of these lines that his own life might be a fiction, in which he was the leading or an accessory character. He happened at the time to be in his study attempting to draft the opening pages of a new short story; its general idea had preoccupied him for some months along with other general ideas, but certain elements of the conceit, without which he could scarcely proceed, remained unclear.

Barth's story offers its rewards, to be sure, as it continues to double back on itself in this dizzying fashion, page after page. It stages a positive tour de force, and Barth is by no means devoid of humor. Hyperaware of his every move, the "author" of the "life story" becomes paralyzed as he concocts one scenario after another, only to find them all, in the end, too dissatisfying. The man desperately wants to write a realistic, rousing, straight-ahead tale, but the more he calculates, the more reasons he finds why this can never be.

The problem with this method of writing (Barth's, that is)

is that it quickly reaches a point of diminishing returns. Because it remains almost purely "about" itself, this metafictional process scarcely leaves breathing room for anything else. In Barth's novels, a semblance of story is always to be had, but the self-referential quality almost always remains in the foreground. His fiction provides intellectual excitement, as you read each page to see whether he can top the preceding one, and he does, and does again, and does again. In some respects, Barth is stunningly proficient.

Yet Barth's failing lies not so much in lack of story as lack of tone. For all his comic bravado, in one enormous novel after another, one finds precious little of the warmth and capaciousness Kundera provides. Both of them are chiefly satirists, but Barth's tone sounds in the end too brittle to be tolerated at length. What dazzles in short form becomes wearisome when transposed into novel form. Kundera engages in genial bullying, but Barth's bullying, while usually high-spirited, could not easily be described as genial. Too often, the "life story" appears to be in pursuit of nothing so much as the sharpening of its own ability to cajole.

> The reader! You dogged, uninsultable, print-oriented bastard, it's you I'm addressing, who else, from inside this monstrous fiction. You've read me this far, then? Even this far? For what discreditable motive? How is it you don't go to a movie, watch TV, stare at a wall, play tennis with a friend, make amorous advances to the person who comes to your mind when I speak of amorous advances? Can nothing surfeit, saturate you, turn you off? Where's your shame?

The first time "the reader" comes across such a passage, there is a willingness to participate in this game, for the sheer novelty of it. In fiction, as in life, there are a lot of us who will try anything once. But because a larger aim doesn't clearly present itself, then the second, and third, and fourth time this trick is played, amusement will likely give way to annoyance. And annoyance is not a luxury a fiction writer, even a brilliant and talented one, can easily afford. One kind of tone dares a reader to continue; another kind invites, persuades, seduces a reader into doing so. Barth belongs to the first category; Kundera to the second.

OMNISCIENT AND PERSONAL

In composing "Garden Springs," the first section of my novel *Kentuckiana,* I tried to put these lessons into practice. The novel relates the adventures of the inhabitants of a subdivision in Lexington, Kentucky, over the course of two decades. I conceived the idea for this section of the novel after a friend of mine complained one day that for writers of our generation, culture had become so homogenous that we didn't have available to us the sort of distinctive growing-up experiences that writers of previous generations enjoyed. All our cultures had become more or less the same. I disagreed, and said that no matter where you grow up, your experiences will always in some way remain different from those of the next writer, no matter how many strip malls and Burger Kings dot the landscape. Though I admired Barth's technique, the last thing I wanted was to end up like his protagonist, paralyzed about writing my own "life story."

I decided to use, for *Kentuckiana*'s first section, a self-confident narrator like one of those in the big novels of the eighteenth and nineteenth century—George Eliot's *Middlemarch,* Jane Austen's *Pride and Prejudice,* Henry Fielding's *Tom Jones* and, of course, Laurence Sterne's *Tristram Shandy*—to suggest that the present time could be as "epic" in its own way as previous centuries. Knowing that living in a little subdivision in central Kentucky was by no means the same thing as inhabiting a manor in England, I opted for a mock-epic tone, one that would come off as both serious and comic, thereby giving me plenty of latitude.

Drawing on metafiction, I called the narrator of "Garden Springs" not by his Christian name, but by his technical name: "the omniscient narrator." Further, I gave him the persona of a planning consultant for the development of my fictional subdivision. I appointed him to be the "god" of this little suburban Garden of Eden. Thus, he would be able to tell the story with comic breadth and gusto, like the narrators of old, but would also possess the kind of modern self-consciousness that we tend to associate with narrators in the twentieth century.

When the omniscient narrator/planning consultant begins to speak of the creation of the subdivision, his tone allows him, to some extent, to have it both ways. He can parody the kind of magnificient biblical language associated in Genesis with the creation of a world, and at the same time, express affection for the little demimonde that he has been appointed to oversee.

Before long, squares of seed-grass were being rolled out onto the barren dirt of future front lawns, the lampposts were in place that Stephen and his friends would shinny up to hang out over the street and shout at passing cars, the blacktop driveways were graded whose tar would turn soft as fresh oatmeal cookies in the summer sun, the manhole covers with the comforting legend Sanitary Sewer were fitted snugly into place, trees were planted as abundant, if not as varied, as the names of the streets they lined: Oleander, Palms, Juniper, Winterberry, Tamarack, Balsam, Cypress, Larkspur, Azalea, Violet, Lily. The crosswalks were painted where Safety Patrol guards would soon stand, wearing orange fluorescent vests and white sashes emblazoned with a metal badge.

Many readers can identify with growing up in a "nondescript" subdivision where the few available scrawny trees contrast with the pretentiously bucolic names on the street signs. And yet, even in such meager surroundings, the life lived by the dwellers there can rival the vitality of the Tom Joneses and Tristram Shandys of another century. You don't have to live in a manor house to feel the intensity of your own existence.

The combination of tone and point of view here allows me the latitude to be both encompassing and intimate, as well as both serious and comic, as long as an underlying affection and tolerance for my fictional creations is palpable in the story's tone. The narrator "inhabits" each of the minds of the different family members one by one, alternating this movement with more general comments about the neighborhood. Having the omniscient narrator assume the point of view of Constance Miles, the family's mother, lets her fret about her gifted but somewhat neurotic son.

> He'd spent much of his time in the past few months indoors and alone, reading entirely too many comic books. When she'd tried to take him outside to teach him herself to throw a baseball, he got scared and ducked, with the result that the baseball knocked him upside the head and he started to cry. Then, when she'd taken him for a visit to a child psychologist, which wasn't cheap, the woman had the nerve to tell her that the problem wasn't Stephen's fear of baseballs, but her insistence on teaching him to play catch.

The passage conveys Constance's guilt and her determination. At the same time, the narrator uses this piece of information to explain why the Miles family chose to move into the subdivision. Before long, the planning consultant has shifted gears, going on to give a comic overview of the new neighbors, and his tone of controlled enthusiasm and gentle irony about the subject makes it easier for him to accomplish this transition from being "in Constance's head" to giving a more sweeping and opinionated view of Garden Springs.

> At the end of the street Jimbo Shaver lives with three people: his mother, a divorced sometime waitress who likes to shack up with policemen only; his grandmother, the oldest private nursing assistant in Lexington, who dyes her hair a black as fierce and forbidding as her own personality; and his grandfather. The latter, stertorously fat, spends most of his time in an easy chair filling and refilling a spittoon, or in the back yard tending his small but beautiful orchard and making jug wine that Jimbo and Stephen will sample at a later date.

Again, the passage helps to continue developing the character of Stephen and the family, while creating the atmosphere and setting of the neighborhood in which many of the novel's crucial events will take place.

A story could be described as a mood that is established, and then gradually, subtly shifted, pulling the reader along with it. When the weather changes by degrees, you may not notice it, especially if you're sitting outdoors at a table in the café where Tamina works, and you're absorbed in the conversation of a friend. You've been telling the friend a few intimate details about your checkered love life, which you feel would make for a pretty good novel. The friend responds by saying "That's just like me, I . . .," and then going on at length about her own love life, which isn't going so well either. The sun keeps pushing its way out from behind a small but stubborn black cloud and before you know it, you've taken off your jacket, rolled up your sleeves, and ordered another cold beer. The weather has you right where it wants you. And, if your friend knows anything about atmosphere and tone, so does she.

Exercises

1. Write a one-page description of an unpopulated landscape. Describe it in such a way that it evokes a particular mood. Now, rewrite the description, this time including a human presence. Don't have the character speak. Let the character simply perceive the surroundings. The description should convey the character's state of mind.

2. Create a two-page "metafictional" monologue in which you, the author, comment on the protagonist you are in the process of making up. See how possible it is to provide a complete characterization while also "digressing" in the style of Kundera. Afterward, subtract out the authorial commentary to see what you are left with, and what difference it makes to the piece you have written.

3. Write a sketch in which you try to control events as much as possible purely through tone. Taking your cue from Cortázar, put the emphasis on establishing atmosphere rather than simply moving events along. Once you have successfully established the atmosphere and tone, you'll find it much easier to expand the sketch into a full-fledged story.

CHAPTER 4

THE VOICE IN DIALOGUE

DIALOGUE IS THE ESSENCE OF TEACHING. It may not be the most efficient route to knowledge, but at its best it becomes, as a colleague of mine once put it, the most "progressively detonating." The act of dialogue sinks in and deepens over time, creating new layers of meaning, so that a person may continue to learn from a lesson long after it has officially ended. The motion of dialogue, beyond its particular content, leaves a whirring in the ear, a restlessness, a dissatisfaction, a desire to say what has been left unsaid and to hear what has been left unheard. And when students, years after a class, have forgotten the specific details of the subject matter, they will remember that process of mutual engagement, if it was indeed real, rather than a setup.

The role of dialogue within fiction can be defined as not so different from the one it plays in learning. Ideally, it should deepen with progressive readings, leaving the reader with an increased understanding of the story's consequences. It can't afford to read as phony, even though, strictly speaking, dialogue makes up part of the artifice of fiction writing. Rhetoric, to be sure, has its place in storytelling, especially in the way it plays off description and supplements it. (This matter will be dealt with more fully in chapter eight, in the difference between descriptive and discursive voices.) But dialogue will seldom convince anyone if it comes across as a series of rhetorical statements and rhetorical questions indirectly posed by the author to "answer" for character. To some extent, it has to succeed independent of the authorial voice.

Characters are authorial creations, of course, and without a doubt the author is given the upper hand and lots of leeway in creating the definitive field of meaning that will be inhabited by the characters. But the characters, when they speak, are not the author's patsies. Even though I am speaking largely in terms of voice in these pages, ventriloquy, if thought of simply as the throwing of one's voice, offers a flawed metaphor and model for the prerogatives of the author to supply dialogue to his imaginary beings.

There's a very good reason why Edgar Bergen (and most of the ventriloquists after him), when he felt the desire to engage in ventriloquy, used the likes of Charlie McCarthy as his dummy. McCarthy can best be described as insolent, smirking and given to talking back. He forces his supposed master to play the role of straight man, while he gets off all the witticisms. Bergen realized that this simple reversal of roles held great appeal for his audiences, because at bottom, most people don't enjoy the particular sleight of hand involved in foisting your opinions on someone by means of an unsuspecting shill. Audiences want to be taken in, without question, but in a way that doesn't leave them feeling like dupes.

Characters in dialogue exist in a state of tension with the authorial self put forward in the story. One might say that characters, to some degree, have an independent existence, caring less about their creator's life story than about the possibilities of their own. They keep the fiction from becoming a thinly veiled biography of the author. This need for tension is especially pressing when characters are conceived in one way or another as the writer's alter egos.

While two or more characters are talking to one another, they are, in a sense, at the same time talking back at the author, making the narrative perspective more complex. This point has considerable significance, since for most writers, their characters end up being an amalgam of various persons they have met, heavily laced with imagination, but almost always leavened with a greater or lesser amount of the writer's own "self." And if the self is everywhere in the story to a greater or lesser degree, then some checks must be provided to ensure that the creating ego doesn't overwhelm the story.

It is just as naive to believe that you are absent from your characters as to believe that you can be simply and transparently represented in fiction. Part of you always resides in your characters, but it is impossible to create, within any given character, a single autobiographical persona that exists completely continuous with who you actually are. Some authors, such as Marcel Proust in *Remembrance of Things Past,* have come close, but even they could not eliminate the distance—at least infinitesimal and sometimes enormous—between author and authorial persona.

READING AROUND THE AUTHOR

Wayne Booth, the author of *The Rhetoric of Fiction,* has said that the "implied author" is not the author's "real self," but should instead be considered a selective and somewhat idealized version—smarter, better, more understanding—than living beings usually tend to be. But no matter how wise and comprehensive this authorial voice, how far-flung, how omniscient, how scattered through the story's landscape, it cannot completely contain the character voices when the characters speak in dialogue. Just as the authorial and narrative voices allow us to read "around" a character (one who is evil, lying or lacking in intelligence, for instance), so character dialogue also allows us, in a sense, to read around the authorial voice. Although the authorial voice may have the last word, it doesn't have all the words.

One of the innovations of modern fiction has been the predilection for putting events largely in scene, that is, relying almost exclusively on cold description and dialogue to convey the meaning of events, and relying little on the direct interpretive capability of the narrator. When the story is in scene, the narrator's or implied author's perspective remains more muted, and can only be conveyed indirectly. This allows the character speaking dialogue to assert herself without having the story immediately and openly interpret what has been said.

It is in this sense that I speak of the character's capacity to talk back to the author. The dialogue, while not freestanding, is not completely enmeshed in the narrative voice either. Of course, one could take this technique too far. This has been the flaw of many of the so-called "minimalist" writers, in which the narrator at times seems absent or, if not absent, less intelligent than the characters being described. It doesn't do to have your characters running the show completely, especially if most of what they have to say is less than fully articulate.

Nonetheless, it serves a purpose to give oneself enough leverage that the dialogue serves as a way to read around the narrator, and to foreground the narrator's varying degrees of reliability. Otherwise, we might as well simply limit ourselves to writing first-person stories in which the narrator is a barely disguised version of the author's own voice. Much of the pleasure, for author and reader, lies in trying out many different kinds of narrators and character voices in dialogue. But the author does not have to be domineering in order to create the effects that he desires. Even when the author wants to preach, or wants to be confessional, the role of character dialogue is, among other things, to contest that impulse. This constraint is the equivalent of putting an egg timer on the preacher's podium, so that he only gets to temporize in three-minute bursts.

PREACHING TO THE CONVERTED

There is a perfectly good reason why the injunction came about in fiction against being "preachy." (Readers seem to have a higher tolerance for confessional fiction, but maybe that's because most of us find it so much easier to hear someone dish dirt on our fellow creatures than to be lectured by them.) It's not that people aren't willing to listen to demagogues and charlatans in real life. Indeed, there seems to be no upper limit to the rhetoric listeners are willing to swallow when it comes to actual demagogues and charlatans. But, just as the servant is accustomed to mocking his master in public with impunity during Carnival, so even the most passive readers, when they turn to fiction, give way to a festive mood of insolence.

Punch and Judy shows may have been barbarous, but the creators of them, in letting both of the puppets wield clubs to punctuate what they were saying to each other, certainly understood the basic principles of entertainment. Nor did they underestimate the audience's need to participate and vociferate. The common reader has been given a bad rap in contemporary times. The common reader may be a little too video literate for his own good, and therefore has an overdeveloped taste for action and fast-paced and predictable plots.

But he, contrary to popular opinion, is for the most part not simply a dolt who wants to be spoonfed ideas. The skepticism on the part of editors about the possibility of publishing "philosophical" novels is understandable but misplaced. Those who still read fiction with any literary pretensions are perfectly willing to entertain ideas, as long as the ideas, in turn, entertain them. The escape that many readers seek in fiction is the escape from having ideas portioned out to them wholesale, in bulk. Like the customer in the Persian carpet store, they want to be wooed and pampered before they buy the dry goods.

Even if it costs them more per yard, they want to have their opinions solicited, after a fashion. Or if they are to be told what to do, this act must be performed in the most solicitous and placating way, if sir or madam would care to step into our private showroom, where the most exquisite samples may be fondled at leisure, and no, no, perish the thought, we have all the time in the world, certainly madam is completely within her rights to want to inspect the one with the plush nap and crimson and azure border, to make comparisons, to set one fabric against another, to believe in the possibility, for a tantalizing instant, that one of the carpets could turn out to be a flying carpet, and the gentleman, too, must be settled in his mind that the fabric of silk and the fabric of imagination are inextricably intertwined, for all intents and purposes one and the same, so that he, through his own free and independent path of discovery and choice, will arrive at the best of all possible rugs. Those who in one context will allow themselves to be manipulated straight out, in another context will insist on exercising their prerogatives, and making you, the author, resort to all sorts of delicious and unnecessary subterfuges. When your characters speak dialogue to one another, they'll have a way of not always getting to the point.

DIALOGUE AS CHARACTER BACKTALK

Grace Paley, whom I've already mentioned in another context, understands this necessity well. In her story "A Conversation With My Father," she stages a dialogue between an alter ego—a writer deliberately modeled after herself—and that woman's father. Because she is using a thinly veiled version of herself in the story, she remains highly conscious of the need to employ comic dialogue to provide a foil for her "authorial" way of seeing things. The conversation, naturally, is about how to tell a proper story. The literate, cantankerous father takes his daughter to task for not telling a plain, simple story, the way Chekhov or one of the other Russian masters would have told it. He wonders aloud why, in his daughter's stories, people seem to have endless conversations that don't resolve anything. "A Conversation With My Father," naturally, mimics the motion of just the kind of tale the father objects to, and so he unwittingly becomes a character in a story he would never consent to being a part of. His objections to her style land him smack in the middle of her tale, as if she'd said to him, "If you don't like the way I'm going about this yarn, then you spin it."

The daughter, half trying to please and placate her father, and half being smartalecky, proceeds to rattle off a bare-bones anecdote about a woman who becomes a junkie in order to identify more closely with her junkie son, who in the end abandons her in disgust. But the father is having none of it. He accuses her of deliberately misunderstanding him.

> "I object not to facts but to people sitting in trees talking senselessly, voices from who knows where . . ."
> "Forget that one, Pa, what have I left out now? In this one?"

"Her looks, for instance."

"Oh. Quite handsome, I think. Yes."

"Her hair?"

"Dark, with heavy braids, as though she were a girl or a foreigner."

"What were her parents like, her stock? That she has become such a person. It's interesting, you know."

"From out of town. Professional people. The first to be divorced in their county. How's that? Enough?" I asked.

"With you, it's all a joke," he said. "What about the boy's father? Why didn't you mention him? Who was he? Or was the boy born out of wedlock?"

"Yes," I said. "He was born out of wedlock."

"For Godsakes, doesn't anyone in your stories get married? Doesn't anyone have the time to run down to City Hall before they jump into bed?"

"No," I said. "In real life, yes. But in my stories, no."

For Paley, fiction has to be not simply true to life, but truer than life. It has to crystallize experience by capturing its essence, but also by giving us more than one way of thinking about that experience. In this case, dialogue serves her desire well. She incorporates opposing viewpoints, managing both to tell the story she wants to tell, one true to her own experience, and another one at cross purposes to hers. The father's story is just as legitimate as hers, in its own way, and though she mildly satirizes his interrogation of her, the story also implies respect, since it is, at bottom, a homage to the father. She can only get at the essence of him, and her love for him, by conjuring him in this adversarial way.

She uses the figure of her father as a verbal sparring partner, one who expresses paternal concern and paternal scorn in the same breath. His objections force her to articulate the precepts by which she lives and writes. I have never understood how the "Socratic method" came to be revered as a model for teaching, since it so obviously falsifies how authentic dialogue between human beings unfolds. Socrates surrounds himself with yes-men, cognitive patsies, and then arrives at a "logical" answer that is, in truth, nothing more than a preestablished effect. Whatever inroads the Socratic method may have made as a pedagogical model, it remains unsuitable for fiction, which is the enactment of human conflict in words.

The saving grace of Paley's story is that she portrays the father not only with gentle mockery, but with obvious pleasure. The proverb that the fruit never falls far from the tree is proven in these pages. His appealing willfulness gets matched by hers. Though they are cast as antagonists, they play off one another beautifully, precisely by not agreeing. And though she speaks her inventions as if to spite him, they follow directly from the questions he asks about the invented female character's appearance and marital status. Earlier in "A Conversation With My Father," the narrator gives a rationale for the way she tells her stories.

> I say "Yes, why not? That's possible." I want to please him, though I don't remember writing that way. I *would* like to try to tell such a story, if he means the kind that begins: "There was a woman . . ." followed by plot, the absolute line between two points which I've always despised. Not for literary reasons, but because it takes all hope away. Everyone, real or invented, deserves the open destiny of life.

TALKING YOUR SWEET TIME

A writer would do well to observe Paley's injunction about allowing fictional characters "the open destiny of life." Sometimes we are too quick to close off avenues for our characters, or to make a passage of dialogue serve too neat or predictable a purpose to "advance" the story. By all means dialogue should be dramatic in intention, as Henry James has advised, but there also can be a certain open-endedness, without its causing any negative effect on the enveloping action. In fact, if you subordinate dialogue too much to your tale's overarching needs, it can begin to sound downright didactic. Take your time, and see how it feels. Human speech, when handled artfully, becomes a pleasure in its own right. There is no reason whatsoever that a passage of dialogue cannot allow itself to become selectively dilatory. There is no immutable law decreeing that every piece of prose must be performed in a brisk and efficient style. If anything, contemporary fiction has tended too far in that direction, to the point that, as Flannery O'Connor once quipped, the short story is in danger of dying of sheer competence.

I have a cousin who lives in Chicago, right off Belmont, about twenty minutes away from me, the only other male of my generation who bears the same last name as myself. Though we grew up hundreds of miles apart, and though neither of us hails from Chicago, we somehow arrived at the same place by distinctly different paths. I call him Cuz, 'cuz I like him a lot, and also because he could easily be one of those varlets in Shakespeare who wanders onstage for thirty seconds between two important scenes with one of his pals in tow, the two of them holding a whimsical and cryptic conversation that doesn't seem to follow strictly from the play's dramatic requirements.

"Indeed, coz, an he were a cuckoo, I'd salt him aright." "E'en so; he were a cockerel, to be spurred so." I've never believed for an instant that Christopher Marlowe wrote any of Shakespeare's plays. But I've always suspected that some inspired hack with mischief in mind penned those indecipherable scenes with the wandering varlets in the margins for a lark, while Shakespeare was away from the desk directing and acting in one of his own shows. It serves him right for trying to be a triple threat.

Whenever my cousin and I get together at his apartment, we spend a lot of time in dialogue, usually standing in his tiny kitchen, or me sitting to one side of the stove on a bar stool, because Cuz is a gourmet cook. "Gourmet" means just about any cuisine he sets his sights on, including the ones requiring whisks and several sauces bubbling on the stovetop at once, although his decided preference is for down-home cooking, peasant food prepared with the same meticulous care he would bring to a French pastry assembled from scratch.

When he makes chili, for instance, he uses three kinds of meat—veal, lamb, and a good cut of stew beef, all of which has to be cubed into different textures, and added to the pot at different times of the day. And, naturally, he makes his own combination of chili powder, the house blend. The longer the meal takes, the more trips he has to make to various speciality groceries in the neighborhood, the greater the number of times he has to return to the refrigerator, and the better he likes it. If he hasn't wasted a considerable amount of time interspersing his concoctions with conversation, the experience doesn't sit quite right with him. He's as liberal with his words as he is with the palm that measures out the spices.

I like to cook too, but I'd much rather sit on the bar stool by the stove watching him chop and stir, taking in gusts of the deepening aroma each time he removes the lid from the iron pot to add yet another ingredient to the simmering stew, and I listen to his disquisition on the most recent court news. Cuz is trained as an attorney, and even worked for a while ghostwriting the opinions of a famous retired federal judge who still freelanced in the Las Vegas courts. But my cousin gave up practicing litigation law after a short time, in part because he's disillusioned with the judicial system, and in part because he'd rather have a humble income, do research, and be able to keep his passions intact—cooking, playing guitar and ukelele, writing songs and science fiction stories.

"What bothers me about the Supreme Court's revised position on search and seizure," he says, "is that we've reached a point where the citizenry just can't wait to hand over its constitutional rights in great steaming hunks."

"Great steaming hunks. You're right," I reply, popping a slice of raw mushroom into my mouth, though I'm already formulating an objection in my mind. "Yes, Cuz, but civil sloth is not something peculiar to our times. Most societies are conservative in nature. We only like to think of ourselves as more enlightened than our predecessors."

"Ah, if that were really so," he retorts, "I could go ahead and open a bierstube for the tragically hip on Halsted Street, and profit from it. I'd call it the Nosh Pit. American law has given us innovations that never existed under Roman law. Look at the gains of the labor movement through the twenties

and thirties. Most of us just don't bother to exercise our civil
liberties.''

"Nosh, pish. You know hipster is the antithesis of radical,
now more than ever. They may listen to industrial rock at the
Metro, but this isn't Liverpool. There ain't no industry. There's
no working class in America anymore, strictly speaking. It's a
sign without a referent. Those guys aren't even lumpens.''

"I don't expect radicalism. Did anybody here hear me use
the word radicalism? Even the people who tap my phone for a
living after they got laid off as phone solicitors for Greenpeace
have never, ever heard that word cross my lips. I just wish the
tragically hip would read the Miranda statement *before* they ram
their heads through those plate glass windows.''

When he turns to the counter to slice serrano chiles length-
wise into threads, I take advantage of the opening, and sample
some of the chili out of the wooden spoon. Then I give the pot
a couple of stirs.

"Hey, hey. Put that spoon down.''

"I was only tasting.''

"You weren't only tasting. Tasting is fine. You were stirring.
No member of our family can pass a stove in somebody else's
house without stirring the pot.''

"I was just checking the chili for lumpens.''

DIALOGUE AND NARRATIVE RESTRAINT

But I digress, don't I? I didn't mean to suggest, by using Paley's
story as an example, that an author has to build an obvious
opponent into his or her pages. I do mean to say, however, that
character dialogue is, by its very nature, agonistic. Characters
speak, in essence, because they disagree, even when they agree
to disagree, or because they have a quarrel with themselves or
the world. This is the case even in the smoothest of narrative
structures, such as the stories of Colette, populated by suave
sophisticates and bon vivants.

Colette builds her stories around dialogue, which then has
to perform most of the work usually relegated to description.

There is plenty of atmosphere in her stories, but the setting for the most part gets sketched in quickly. She understands that description works by selection, not accumulation. In "The Other Wife," a newlywed couple enters a posh restaurant for lunch. In the brief course of events, we discover that he has been married before, and that his ex-wife is seated in the same restaurant, having lunch. The dialogue, like the description, remains spare, in contrast to Paley's kvetching, boisterous exchanges. This spareness has everything to do with the social milieu occupied by Colette's characters. Everything must remain understated, polite, under one's breath, so as not to betray an inappropriate excess of emotion.

So it is that when Marc spots his ex-wife across the room, on his way to the table, he reacts toward his new wife in a brusque but skillful and relatively silent manner.

> Her husband caught her by passing his arm under hers. "We'll be more comfortable over there."
> "There? In the middle of all those people? I'd much rather . . ."
> "Alice, please."
> He tightened his grip in such a meaningful way she turned around. "What's the matter?"
> "Shh . . ." he said softly, looking at her intently, and led her toward the table in the middle.
> "What is it, Marc?"
> "I'll tell you, darling. Let me order lunch first. Would you like the shrimp? Or the eggs in aspic?"
> "Whatever you like, you know that."

Note the brevity of Colette's paragraphs. I normally discourage my beginning students from using too-brief paragraphs, and from relying heavily on dialogue without situating it within an adequate descriptive context. But here, on both counts, Colette is within her rights, since she makes her dialogue do the work of exposition and description, without calling attention to the fact. Within a few exchanges, the readers have been comfortably seated, so to speak, within the story, and possess a clear understanding of the dramatic situation. Likewise, the relation between the two principal characters has been defined with sufficient clarity. The single exchange regarding the meal lets us know, in short order, that he is the experienced one, and she the ingenue.

One might think that this method would preclude the kind of agon or conflict through dialogue that I spoke of earlier with regard to Paley's story. But not so. Colette's "The Other Wife" examines the muted, subterranean conflicts of a social class that doesn't allow itself to display its problems or domestic conflicts in public. It is no accident that Colette sets this encounter in a public place. Neither we nor they can forget for a moment that they are sitting "in the middle of all those people." Marc and Alice must show restraint in their dialogue. The tone of their conversation becomes half-intimate, half-understated. The dialogue can be described as stylized but highly realistic, that combination of brazenness and reserve that characterizes the peculiar way people talk in restaurants about their personal lives, all the more so when they're used to obeying a code of honor that frowns on gaudy displays of emotion—less because of the morality involved than because displays are rude.

Marc and Alice think of themselves as cool, sophisticated, in control of themselves. Despite the presence of "the other wife," they have resolved to remain adult about the uncomfortable situation. Yet the longer they speak, and the more Marc discloses about his former marriage, the more their anxieties bubble up to the surface, like effervescent champagne that hasn't been touched, and is on the point of losing its sparkle and turning flat.

> "Incompatibility," Marc said. "Oh, I mean . . . total incompatibility! We divorced like well-bred people, almost like friends, quietly, quickly. And then I fell in love with you, and you really wanted to be happy with me. How lucky we are that our happiness doesn't involve any guilty parties or victims!"
>
> The woman in white, whose smooth, lustrous hair reflected the light from the sea in azure patches, was

smoking a cigarette with her eyes half closed. Alice turned back toward her husband, took some shrimp and butter, and ate calmly. After a moment's silence she asked: "Why didn't you ever tell me that she had blue eyes too?"

Colette uses dramatic irony—that is, irony deriving from the situation—to good effect in this passage. At various times the characters have expostulated about how the other wife's presence has no effect on them ("She's the one who must be uncomfortable."), and yet their entire conversation revolves around her. It is a mark of Colette's ingenuity that the other wife barely exists as a character in the story, and yet she reposes at its center, "smoking a cigarette with her eyes half closed."

The parameters of this episode don't allow for any open conflict between Marc and Alice, who think of themselves as "well-bred people," and yet Marc's description of the unspoken rift in his former marriage, leading to a quick and quiet divorce, implies that trouble may develop soon in the worshipful paradise of his current marriage. One watches the current blue-eyed wife's attitude subtly mutate from adoration to suspicion in the course of a single outwardly placid meal.

Colette exploits the disparity between Marc's superficial worldliness and Alice's naïveté at the story's end, when the newlywed wife experiences a small epiphany, realizing that in the eyes of "the other wife," this husband might not be such a catch after all, in spite of his self-possession before a menu. By the final sentence, she gazes "with envy and curiosity at the woman in white, this dissatisfied, this difficult, this superior."

THE GOSSIP EFFECT

Dialogue dominates "The Other Wife," as I have mentioned. This technique holds the third-person narrator in abeyance, and makes the authorial presence appear, at one and the same time, both sharp and muted. The story benefits from what I call "the gossip effect," which is normally created by means of giving a reader access to a character's diary entry, or a letter written to someone else in the story. Our prurient curiosity, if nothing else, draws us to the encounter. Here, it is as though we were seated at the next table over from this couple, overhearing their intimate conversation without interference. The narration largely restricts itself to selecting the dialogue the two will speak, and only at crucial points, such as after Marc's recitation of the divorce, does it indulge in a couple of sentences of straight description.

If we think of dialogue, therefore, as tantamount to description in this case, then Caroline Gordon and Allen Tate's definition of the "concealed narrator," in *The House of Fiction*, allows us to better understand the relation I began this chapter with: that existing between the dialogue and the authorial presence. The concealed narrator doesn't appear as a character within the story. On the contrary, its goal is to make itself as invisible as possible, while strongly shaping the coherence of descriptive passages and setting limits on possible interpretations of them. Rather than guiding our eye to itself, the concealed narrator tries to make us see what it wants us to see. Nothing should openly distract us from the flow of experience within the story. As Gordon and Tate point out, with the use of the concealed narrator,

> the dead lumps of description, the mere *telling* what happened, the summaries and inert reports of information about persons and places disappear, or rather they are actively *rendered* in relation to what the characters are feeling and doing. . . . The reader has to know more about the central character than he knows about himself in order to understand the story.

When the matter is put in this way, one can begin to comprehend how remarkably calculated an effect Colette creates, despite the seeming artlessness of her prose. She makes her dialogue yield up a great deal by investing it with dramatic irony through the use of a concealed narrator. We understand the submerged distress in Alice's questions better than she does herself. To return to my earlier phrase, Marc's spoken words and the presence of the other woman have a "progressively detonating" effect on her, such that by the story's end, she has only begun to intuit the full consequences for herself of her husband's previous marriage. It is part conjecture to believe that this couple, too, will end up divorced, but the story, without overtly stating it, leaves that open as a distinct possibility.

I want to reiterate that Colette's dialogue stands as the antithesis to "the mere *telling* what happened" deplored by Gordon and Tate. That is why I define dialogue as a function of description, of the kind that does not consist of "inert summaries and reports." One of my most challenging tasks as a teacher is to get my students thinking about dialogue as a comprehensive element of fiction. Because of the easy fluency of most students in movie-speak, I often have to point out that what they are actually writing, when they turn in pages of inert character conversation, is movie dialogue, or the kinds of verbal back-and-forth that one might find in a television screenplay.

Though I am a movie aficionado myself, and though many films have been adapted from novels, the style of film and television dialogue simply does not transfer to the writing of a short story or novel. At first blush, a script might seem to offer itself as an appropriate model, since a film script consists almost entirely of dialogue, except for instructions regarding visual cues such as camera angles. The problem, however, lies in the fact that in most movies, the screenplay becomes subordinated to spectacle. Screenplays locate the actors within the action and within somewhat preordained character relationships, for which the dialogue serves more as an illustration or complement, rather than creating those relationships. Or, to the extent that screenplays do create character, they depend on the fact that a visual presence, an actual image of a talking person, will appear before the viewer, and that the voice will be a recording of a real one.

The principles of stage plays are slightly more transferable, since the playwright's text historically has had primacy, rather than being subordinated to the element of spectacle. Yet the playwright and actors both have an equal hand in creating the text's total meaning at the moment of performance. In this respect, playwrights, like screenwriters, must hypothesize as they write about the performance, factoring in the element of spectacle as they go.

If a playwright or screenwriter (unlike the fiction writer) truly felt that his or her work was finished and self-sufficient once the writing was over, and didn't depend on performance for its completion, then that play or screenplay would probably be a failure. In fiction, the later performance of the words, in the strict sense, does not form part of the writer's working hypothesis. A playwright or screenwriter can afford to be more minimalist and notational in approach than a fiction writer, without the work of art feeling impoverished.

John Fowles, the author of *The French Lieutenant's Woman*, shows an awareness of this difference in his foreword to Harold Pinter's screenplay adaptation of the novel. While admitting that parts of the two domains overlap, he adds that "there are others that are no-go territory; visual things the word can never capture (think, for instance, of the appalling paucity of vocabulary to define the endless nuances of facial expression), and word things the camera will never photograph nor actors ever speak." This interdependence between visual and verbal in screenplays is clear in any number of the scenes in the adaptation of *The French Lieutenant's Woman*. Take, for instance, one of the brief encounters between Ernestina and her maid, Mary.

ERNESTINA *half dressed.* MARY *knocks and enters.*

Mary: Mr. Charles is here, Miss, to see you.
Ernestina: Mr. Charles?
Mary: He's downstairs waiting for you Miss. He wants to speak to you.
Ernestina: Oh dear! What shall I . . . What dress shall I wear?
Mary: Oh your green is so lovely Miss. You look pretty as a picture in green.
Ernestina: Yes, yes. My green. I'll wear that.

If this minimalist dialogue seems simple, it's not because Pinter has written a defective screenplay. On the contrary, he has been careful not to have the dialogue try to perform the total work of artistic creation and impression, the way that Colette does in her story. He may enable the filming in powerful ways, but not pre-empt it. The dialogue is quite ordinary, almost forgettable but not quite. "You look pretty as a picture" doesn't exactly stun us with metaphorical originality. But the means of expression seem adequate to a scene that will depend in part on facial expressions, character interpretation by the two actresses and their mutual rapport, and the impending intimacy and present vulnerability of Ernestina, to be suggested as much as anything by the onscreen image of her half-dressed, being counseled by her maid. If this screenplay were again recast, say, as a short story, the dialogue could not stand pat, because it would read as too thin, too lacking in emotional subtlety. It couldn't, as the screenplay must necessarily do, leave so many things out.

On the whole, it is most useful to think of fiction dialogue as having its own regulating principles. Otherwise, dialogue-rich stories can indeed easily come off sounding like bad screenplays. Point of view, character development and dramatic action are all implied in the handling of fiction dialogue. Keep in mind that both point of view and dialogue are aspects of voice. They exist simultaneously at different levels within the story. Character as well remains bound to considerations of voice—first, because a character is always being narrated by someone (either himself or someone else within the story, or a disembodied narrator), and second, because characters create dialogue through their written "speech." But even though voice, in the end, speaks as a single creative entity, it can remain strategically and selectively at odds with itself, and thereby can create the kinds of multiple meanings and complexity usually associated with dramatic irony—the irony of the story or novel's ground situation, taken as a whole.

DIALOGUE AND THE SINGLE MOMENT

The skillful deployment of dialogue allows that irony to exist for the purposes of the story as a whole, but also within the individual scene as an entity unto itself. Again, the pleasure of the particular instance doesn't always have to subordinate itself to the whole story. The writer of a short story is always after what Edgar Allan Poe called "unity of effect." Still, we read, after all, scene by scene, paragraph by paragraph, utterance by utterance. Thus, in any event, it is only possible to take in the entire story after one has gone through this process of relishing each instance of description, narration and character speech. As I have said before, the writer operates by strict selection, but the reader operates by accumulation.

One of the most graceful yet pungent practitioners of the arresting single moment, with consequences for the entire story, is the Russian writer Isaac Babel. One exemplary instance comes near the end of "Di Grasso," the story of Nick Schwartz, a less than scrupulous theatrical promoter who deals with his underlings in a stingy fashion. One of his ill-paid employees, in a moment of desperation, has pawned his father's watch to Nick, but later Nick, "even with his money back, could still not bring himself to return the watch to me. Such was his character."

After a theater performance, the employee (who is also the story's narrator) walks along in tow of Nick and his wife, who has been moved to tears by the cheap romantic spectacle of the play. At this moment, Babel accomplishes one of his rapid-fire climaxes, in part through telescopic use of dialogue.

> Stomping ponderously, Madam Schwarz moved along Langeron Street; tears rolled from her fishlike eyes, and the shawl with the fringe shuddered on her obese shoulders. Dragging her mannish soles, rocking her head, she reckoned up, in a voice that made the streets re-echo, the women who got on well with their husbands.
>
> " 'Ducky,' they're called by their husbands; 'sweety-pie' they're called . . ."
>
> The cowed Nick walked along by his wife, quietly blowing on his silky mustaches. From force of habit I followed on behind, sobbing. During a momentary pause Madam Schwarz heard my sobs and turned around.
>
> "See here," she said to her husband, her fisheyes

agoggle, "may I not die a beautiful death if you don't give this boy his watch back!"

Nick froze, mouth agape; then came to me and, giving me a vicious pinch, thrust the watch at me sideways.

The tableau rapidly becomes vivid. The three characters constitute an unusual ménage à trois. The employee retrieves the watch, in effect, on account of Nick's marital shortcomings. As an ersatz "lover," he snatches from Nick his most cherished possession—not the wife, but the watch. Babel, a master of irony, makes this little scene yield up all of its dramatic possibilities. The scene in the street looks even more tawdry than the melodrama they've just finished seeing. At the same time, circumstance forces the unwilling Nick to disgorge the contents of his meretricious character to the reader. Like his employee, we too are wresting something from him.

This effect is achieved in part through Babel's way of using dialogue. " 'Ducky,' they're called by their husbands; 'sweety-pie' they're called . . ." Madame Schwarz's dialogue is extravagant but clipped, implying that she's been talking to him on the same subject for a long time. The ellipsis is nothing short of brilliant. It suggests that she has harangued him for months and years about his shortcomings as a husband and lover. She may go on and on, but Babel doesn't. This instant of dialogue opens, with consequences for the story as a whole, intimating how we are to view the entrepreneur Nick Schwarz. Likewise, with her single pronouncement "May I not die a beautiful death if you don't give this boy his watch back," she presents herself as a third-rate Madame Bovary of the steppes—just the kind of theatrical character that Nick himself specializes in bringing to town. The vividness of her speech and mannerisms keeps our eyes and ears trained on the immediate moment, almost without regard for what has come before and what will come after—this, in spite of the fact that we are witnessing the story's "climax," where all the story's elements presumably come together.

Babel almost always operates through compression—the quick and colorful glimpse, a few memorable, representative details. He prefers the single, pithy descriptive phrase over an accumulation of near misses.

Babel begins by giving particular attention to smaller units of construction, such as the paragraph and the sentence. It is no accident that an ellipsis, a mere bit of punctuation that for most writers would be a throwaway or at best a mechanical pause, for this writer remains pregnant with character revelation. This effect is highly calculated and deliberate on Babel's part. In an interview, he spoke of this predilection.

> I break my texts into easy phrases. The more periods the better. Each phrase is one thought, one image and no more. So don't be afraid of periods. . . . All the paragraphs and punctuation must be done correctly, not out of some dead scholasticism, but so as to produce the maximum effect upon the reader. The paragraph is particularly magnificent. It lets you change rhythms easily and often; like a flash of lightning, it reveals some well-known sight in a completely unexpected aspect.

Take Babel's advice and give sustained attention to your sentence construction. In poetry, the basic unit of composition is the line. In fiction, the basic unit is the sentence. Try writing compact sentences that contain, as Babel says, "one thought, one image and no more." It is easy to avoid monotony by making minor variations in syntax. Be aware of the sentence as an end in itself, rather than as simply a means of getting to the next sentence. Often we are in so much of a hurry to get the story told, we forget to take care with our essential materials, which are words.

SELF-SUFFICIENT AND SELF-CONTAINED

Babel's breaking down of his text, especially his handling of dialogue in scene, in the context of the paragraph, gives rise to another distinction. Most stories are made up of a series of vignettes or episodes. In some cases, the vignettes almost constitute stories within the story. This way of structuring the text can add texture to your writing, and not seem inappropriate. You must, however, ensure that they are self-sufficient, rather than self-contained. A self-contained vignette presents itself as completely freestanding, and thus may appear an unnecessary digression from the story's larger aims. Like the dialogue above, it may seem to exist merely for its own sake, without becoming integrated into the narrative flow.

You can, however, take some liberties. If a vignette seems self-sufficient, that simply means that it has all the elements of a story and is readable and enjoyable for its own sake, while at the same time it proceeds from, and flows to, those scenes that come before and after. It remains part of the story's unity of effect, while also exhibiting a certain showmanship of its own, one that makes it worthy of lingering over.

One such occasion comes in the midst of Babel's renowned "My First Goose," which recounts how a bespectacled, educated soldier ingratiates himself with his oafish Cossack fellow soldiers. At first, they look askance at him, but he becomes one of the boys after degrading himself by snatching a goose from a helpless, ancient peasant woman, stepping on its neck, and ordering her to cook it for him. This act satisfies the mindless, cavalier bloodlust of the Cossacks, and they make room for him around the campfire.

The moment of transition into this scene comes after he has been assigned to his post and turned over to the quartermaster to find a billet for the night. This transition could turn into a weak link in the story, mere business to be hastily performed, like the opening and shutting of doors in a play as characters enter or exit the stage. Babel, however, turns it into a chance to characterize the quartermaster as a cowardly oracle. In a few sentences of dialogue, the quartermaster describes the arc of the story as a whole. Yet his character and manner of speech leave an indelible impression of this cameo appearance within the story.

The quartermaster carried my trunk on his shoulder. Before us stretched the village street. The dying sun, round and yellow as a pumpkin, was giving up its roseate ghost to the skies.

We went up to a hut painted over with garlands. The quartermaster stopped, and said suddenly, with a guilty smile: "Nuisance with specs. Can't do anything to stop it, either. Not a life for the brainy type here. But you go and mess up a lady, and a good lady too, and you'll have the boys patting you on the back."

He hesitated, my little trunk on his shoulder, then he came quite close to me, only to dart away again despairingly and run to the nearest yard. Cossacks were sitting there, shaving one another.

"Here you soldiers," said the quartermaster, setting my little trunk down on the ground. "Comrade Savitsky's orders are that you're to take this chap in your billets, so no nonsense about it, because the chap's been through a lot in the learning line."

The quartermaster, purple in the face, left us without looking back.

Much is divulged in the quartermaster's remarks. When he counsels the soldier to "mess up a lady," he performs, on the one hand, an act of kindness by letting the soldier know exactly what a "brainy type" has to do to survive among this rough bunch. On the other hand, his counsel dooms at least one "lady," to the kind of treatment routinely meted out by the Cossacks. The quartermaster waxes positively Shakespearean (think of Iago) in his ability to condemn an innocent fellow character with a passing remark.

Much the same holds true once they arrive at the billet. In introducing the soldier to his mates, the quartermaster condemns him in earshot of the Cossacks by announcing that "the chap's been through a lot in the learning line." It is possible to interpret the quartermaster as deliberately malicious or simply so nervous, "purple in the face," and cowed by the Cossacks that he can't help speaking idiocies. Just as the complexities of his character begin to multiply, he disappears.

This vignette is self-sufficient, offering depth and dimensionality, but it is not self-contained. It depends directly on the animating presence of the Cossacks, and in terms of structure, represents a segue, a transition into that scene. All the same, because of the canny use of dialogue, the vignette succeeds on its own terms, while providing a savvy setup for the narrator's encounter with "My First Goose."

Dialogue means much more than a character talking. Speech is a pleasure in its own right, and characters that serve as mere mouthpieces for the story's content will not sustain interest for long. Yet keep in mind that a line of dialogue can be explosive beyond its occasional content, in terms of its consequences for the story at large. Dialogue should have a "progressively detonating" effect. Like the dynamite cap at the entrance to the sealed-off cave, it contains the potential for all kinds of percussions and repercussions within the story, and can open the way to unsuspected depths, and interior passages whose existence the writer doesn't even suspect.

Exercises

1. Write a scene in which two characters disagree. One of the characters should espouse ideas you feel comfortable with, the other, ones you don't feel comfortable with. Don't stack the deck by making one of the characters a "patsy." Also, keep in mind that this is not a debate. The dialogue should become dramatic rather than didactic. The characters don't have to be tossing around big ideas to be engaging.

2. Create an episode made almost exclusively of dialogue. In this episode, the characters will reveal themselves through understated speech. Make your description minimal. The dialogue itself should be descriptive. The exchange may take place in public, as in Colette's story, or the characters, though speaking in private, may simply be emotionally reserved.

3. Write an entire story in which your emphasis, like Babel's, falls on revealing the "single moment" through a combination of description and dialogue. The story should contain at least two self-sufficient vignettes that still remain an organic part of the story as a whole.

CHAPTER 5

DIALECT AND VOICE

WHEN A FICTION WRITER AIMS TO MAKE DIALECT a part of character dialogue, the first order of business is for the writer to hear what is actually said around him. We become so used to our own speech habits that we start to take them for granted, to the point where we can't even hear the distinctive flavor of the way our neighbors speak. When you want to give your writing a regional or authentic flavor, you don't need to trot out types alien to your experience. Remember that everyone, no matter from what social class or region of the country, speaks in some sort of dialect. No one qualifies as exempt. Standard American English is a myth, a language no one actually uses, except certain newscasters who learn to iron the kinks out of their tongue before they go on the air. Even Dorothy from Kansas knew you didn't have to look any further than your own backyard for a diphthong. And the Wizard, after trying his hand and failing at Emerald-speak, turned out to be "an old Kansas man myself." His vowels gave him away, as they usually do. Therefore, you should turn to your advantage the fact that your native dialect, no matter what part of the country you're from, is rich with fictional possibilities. Use it.

For years, my wife and I kept up a running debate about whether or not she had an accent. In my case, there wasn't much question about the matter, since I hail from Kentucky, descended from rednecks, storekeepers and yeoman farmers. For her, the charms of my speech are the soft elongation of vowels, the upward lilt at the end of certain words, and the way I use only two syllables to speak the word "Louisville," swallowing as I utter it, and hitting down on the first syllable— *Lúuh*-vl. And she can hear easily enough the way the Chicagoans who we live in the midst of give their own special Midwestern nasal twang to that same word, their faces scrunched up against the December gusts off Lake Michigan as if they wish they really were in Louisville, instead of in the Windy City. They say: "I wouldn't mind being in LOO-EEEE-ville right now."

And when one of them makes that wish, her friend who lives on the North Shore will answer, in that turn of phrase unique to her ilk, "Me too. I want to go with." Whenever I hear that singular sentence—*I want to go with*—I keep waiting for the prepositional object to drop, to ask, "With who?" But by now I know the answer. When Chicagoans say "I want to go with," they mean "I want to go with *you*." Especially if it's to Louisville in the middle of winter. Even our daughter, whose speech habits are being formed as much by her playmates as they are by us, wants to go with. Especially if it's to McDonald's or Chuck E. Cheese. Corporate America can take away her ability to taste the flavor of real food, but it can't take away the flavor of her evolving Chicago accent.

My wife, however, hails from Indiana, a land, she claims, with speech habits as flat and indistinct as the land itself. Her ear recognizes the nuances of the Chicago speech and she plucks out the peculiarities of the Kentucky dialect when we make the trip down past *Lúuh*vl to Lexington, because those accents and cadences and figures of speech differ from hers. But in her version of our debate, many is the time she's told me, in no uncertain terms, "I don't have an accent."

In one especially vigorous conversation, she tried to close the matter by announcing, "I speak like Walter Cronkite. And that's the way it is." This, I must say, was news to me. It surprised me more than any of the news ever announced to me by Walter Cronkite in his grandfatherly TV-speak—the invented language that has a lot more in common with Wilford Brimley exhorting me to eat Quaker Oats than it does with either my real grandfather or my wife. I have a soft spot for Wilford, that cuss who cusses about natural cereal in unnatural phonemes. But I'm relieved that my wife, with her Indiana accent, doesn't really talk like him.

When we visit her family, on a rainy Thanksgiving weekend, there's a lot of chat about getting out the *UM*-brellas, so we don't get soaked on the way to the car. The first time I found myself amongst that strange tribe called Hoosiers, and heard them say this, I expected the *UM*-brellas to be unusually large, maybe twice the size of golf umbrellas. But they turned out, disappointingly, to look a lot like the umbrellas of my youth. And a lot different from the umbrellas of Chicago, which, like their vowels, are turned permanently inside out. When it was time for bed, my mother-in-law rushed into the guest bedroom and said "Let me fix that bedspread. It's all *cattywampus.*" I half expected an animal from Dr. Seuss to be lurking under the covers. The seven-humped cattywampus.

But it turns out to mean only that the covers are crooked, twisted, askew. To my wife's ear, the term sounds quite natural. To mine, it sounds all cattywampus. Then again, until a few years ago, she never perceived the softening of *v*'s to *f*'s when her father, a native Dutchman, asked me to pass the fegetables, turn up the folume on the classical music station, or help him change the battery in the Folkswagen. All I know is, the only people who speak the way God meant for them to speak are Kentuckians. All the rest are exotic songbirds.

RENDERING DIALECT

My wife's insistence on her neutral speech is quite natural. But for a fiction writer, it won't do to let the pitch of your kin start to sound normal to your ears. Above all, you have to cultivate an ear for the dialect of your own kind. This doesn't mean, however, to lay it on too thick. There is seldom any need to concoct odd phonetic spellings and load the sentence down with incomprehensible phrases that no one outside East St. Louis, or West Terre Haute, or South San Francisco will be able to understand. A little goes a long way, as long as you've put the right word in the right place. I often remind my creative writing students that dialogue is a representation, not a transcription. The simple meaning of that fancy saying is that when we make our characters speak, we're not trying to be anthropologists or linguists. We don't have to capture letter for letter, sound for sound, each sentence exactly as it was uttered by someone native to the area. The point is to get the distinctive sound of that speech, and a craving for it, into your reader's ear.

Like the performance of a good jazz guitarist, your successful use of dialect in voice doesn't consist in seeing who can cram the most notes into one bar of music. Although Kentucky writer Elizabeth Maddox Roberts excels at the passages of prose description of farm life that she liked to call "poetic realism," she falls down somewhat when she turns her ear to her characters' dialogue. She relies too much on specific, repeated words to telegraph the country accents of her characters. In *The Time of Man*, a house dance party among poor migrant farmers is starting to wind down, and the characters start to get testy with each other.

> "Durned if here ain't a louse," one said.
> "Oh, shut up!"
> "Keep hit to yourself, hit's your'n."
> "Well, it is one, now."
> "Well kill hit then."
> "Hit's a tater bug."
> "Hit's a gnat or a flea, maybe."
> "Flea your hind leg! Hit's a body louse."

The effect of the passage is spoiled because Maddox "hits" down too hard on a single "misspelled" word to define the sensibility of each character, with the result of having them all sound the same. Though it's typical of some areas of Kentucky to add the "h" at the beginning of "it," heavily employing it in this passage has the unfortunate effect of marking all the characters, in a similar way, as hayseeds—exactly what Maddox tries not to do in the novel as a whole. She wants us to respect and admire these honest workers down on their luck.

However, by placing too much emphasis on the regional type, she sacrifices the credibility of individual characters. It has frequently been said that regional fiction fails because it isn't universal enough. But the opposite holds true. If it fails, the blame more often than not lies in the fact that the individual character traits, especially dialect, aren't distinctive enough. The writer goes awry by settling for a stereotype that has just enough elements of truth to it to make the reader disgruntled. Remember that most stereotypes, in a limited sense, have an essence of truth to them. That's how they become stereotypes. But therein lies the danger. If you don't develop enough of an ear to express the subtleties of speech of the kind of characters you want to portray, you can never hope to make your reader see beyond their "typical" traits.

Mastery of voice allows you to characterize "types" who interest you without having them seem utterly predictable. Complex plotting won't save you from this pitfall, nor will throwing the characters into an evocative setting. If setting were a saving grace, then Elizabeth Maddox Roberts's descriptive power, when she speaks of how "the grass was high and full with seeds and the white clover was in bloom—late June," could carry the day for her characters. The beauty of her descriptions could lull one into accepting her vision of western Kentucky at face value. But when her characters begin to speak, our ear begins to question what our eye has accepted. Voice may be the most elusive of the elements of fiction, but only because it is the most crucial. The breath of voice is the breath of life—difficult to grasp at times, but vital.

THE RIGHT WORDS IN THE RIGHT PLACE

Much more accomplished than Roberts's dialogue is James Still's judicious but accurate use of folk speech in "A Master Time," a story about a hog-killing. As Ulysses and John, the two butchers, cut up the hog, their spare dialogue has been well chosen, so that two different things happen at the same time. First, their talk conveys specialized information about hog-killing without having it sound like a researched essay on the subject. Second, James Still, in that same stroke, gives us a clear sense of each man's particular mindset, and of the relationship between the two of them.

> Ulysses and John served as the butchers, and as they labored, John questioned:—
> "Want the lights saved?"
> "Yes, s'r," Ulysses replied.
> "Heart-lump?"
> "Yip."
> "The particulars?"
> "Nay-o."
> "Sweetbreads?"
> "Fling them away and Aunt Besh will rack us. The single part she will eat."

The specialized local words for the parts of the hog: "lights," "heart-lump," "particulars," "sweetbreads," could be used interchangeably by any of the men in the community. But what makes those terms engaging is how they mark out the character of Ulysses, whose land the butchering takes place on, as close-mouthed. Ulysses is a man in a tight spot. He's invited the menfolk and their wives over to help him with the labor of hog-killing, and is bound by local etiquette to offer the men some whisky to repay them for their work. At the same time, the women in the house are dead set against the men drinking, and Ulysses has to answer to those women directly if he goes against their wishes.

As John, his neighbor and helper, asks Ulysses which parts of the hog he wants to keep, and which to throw out, we can see Ulysses, outwardly, trying to give the impression of a man in charge of things, who knows his own mind. At the same time, he says as few words as possible to keep from showing his discomfort, until John teasingly pushes him into a corner by asking him if he wants to keep the sweetbreads, knowing full well that it's Aunt Besh's favorite part of the pig. Ulysses is then forced to admit that what's on his mind, as he says yes or no to each question, is figuring out what will be most pleasing to the women inside, such as Aunt Besh, rather than to himself. Like the pig, the part of himself Ulysses is forced to discard under the circumstances is his "particulars." And that's an uncomfortable fact.

All of this comes across through the use of a few well-chosen and well-placed words of dialect. Note that one doesn't have to know beforehand the specialized meanings of the words. James Still makes their meaning clear enough in the context of the story. We know as much about hog-butchering as we need to know, and no more. And "Yip" and "Nay-o," like the names for the different parts of the hog, are used not for their value as mere local color, but rather to promote the dramatic action—the movement of the story as a whole—and to point to character conflict.

Later on in the story, this conversation resonates even more, after the men have come in and eaten dinner only to discover that their wives have played a trick on them to keep them from their drink.

> While we were at table the wives hid the churn, and when they joined us in the living room later in the evening the four estranged couples sat apart, gibing each other. Ulysses tried making the peace between them. The wives wouldn't budge, though the husbands appeared willing.
>
> John sighed, "Gee-o, I'm thirsty," and his wife asked sourly, "What's against pure water?" "Hit's weaky," was the reply.

Still's single use of the word "hit" in this passage comes out of the mouth of a sole character, who uses it to express his disgust at having been outfoxed by his wife. He doesn't simply pepper the page with it like mountain seasoning for rabbit stew. Still's use of dialect is always ruled by the dramatic concerns of the scene, rather than tacked on for its own sake. When you employ dialect words, always hold yourself to the same standard as you do with the more formal registers of diction you may use when writing third-person fiction. Ask yourself, about each individual word, exactly as you do when you're writing a passage of description, whether it truly justifies its existence within the sentence.

Sometimes writers who are very strict with themselves about editing their third-person narrative voice suddenly become freewheeling and liberal, and turn off their self-editor as soon as they begin to use first-person prose. It's as if they say to themselves, well, the characters are talking now, so I'll just let them talk. Next thing you know, your Ulysses and Aunt Besh will have turned into Jed and Granny Clampett, and they'll be telling all and sundry about how they're fixing to do something or other, how it's high time they did, dadgummit, and how they'll have to go way down yonder to get it done. And by the time you get your wits about you to tell them "Whoa, dogies," the story may already have spun out of control.

DIFFERENT DIALECTS IN THE SAME STORY

In any case, the "regional" characters in a single story or novel won't necessarily even partake of the same way of talking. Their level of education, social class and individual desires may make them express their longings in vocabularies markedly different from one another. Their dialects may be almost mutually unintelligible. In my novel *Kentuckiana*, the different stories in the book are narrated by a total of six narrators, each of whom has a distinctive manner of speaking, in spite of the fact that five of them are members of the same immediate family.

The father of the family, Jean, regrets having separated himself from his rural roots, and he meets the ghost of his father in a holler where they once lived. Jean has just cleared the dead leaves away from a cold spring to take a drink of fresh water. When the ghost of his father, Bart, begins to speak, the sound of his country language coming from beyond the grave is as sweet and refreshing to Jean's ears as the water was to his thirsty mouth.

"Bart," I whispered, not daring to move, or even ex-
hale my smoke too fast. "Is it you?"

"You know, Jean," he said, "I've been hankering after
some of Francine's soup beans with that good chow-chow
she makes. I think about those damn things all the time,
and it like to drives me crazy. You can't get beans like that
nowhere else, can you?"

"No, Dad. I love them too."

Jean hankers after the sound of words like "hanker" and
"chow-chow" the same way that Bart hankers after the actual
taste of beans and chow-chow, pleasures no longer available to
him in the beyond. The relish for words, in this part of the
novel, has to be as strong as the relish for relish, and so it makes
perfect sense to draw on a countryfied Kentucky dialect as a
way of defining the character of Jean and his yearnings.

The use of voice here means much more than the voice of
the character speaking. It refers to the first-person character
retelling, from the vantage point of middle age, a story about
his youth, and the way life's hardships have caused him to miss
opportunities and move further and further away from the person he originally intended to be. One senses a combination of
regret, sorrow, tenderness and stoicism in his manner of
speech. At the same time, even though the story is told in first
person, the voice has to remain roomy enough for the "implied
author"—the larger voice containing the first-person narrator—to give readers clues about how to interpret Jean's actions
and emotions.

Especially when you do have a character in a "dialect"
situation, the use of voice allows you a certain leverage in terms
of respecting the character's intelligence, rather than indulging in folksy overkill. You can actually think "more" than the
character would be able to by himself or herself, and make
language available that he or she wouldn't normally use. Jean,
for instance, speaks about his strained relations with his oldest
daughter, Judy, who used to come to get free food at the restaurant he managed, even at a time when she disliked him intensely. The use of a different, slightly more formal register of

the same character voice lets him express his feelings about Judy without seeming either distant or self-pitying. To strike this balance, he needs to have available to him a more restrained and less broad way of talking, since he is, so to speak, a different man in the city as a restaurant manager than when he's standing in a holler in rural Kentucky speaking to the ghost of his father.

> She never thanked me for any of the meals she ate there. I didn't expect her to; I only wanted her to see that I was doing well, making more money than I ever had, and she was welcome to whatever share of it she could bring herself to ask for. I'd give her twenty or fifty, whatever she requested, and about once a week I filled up her gas tank. When I made my rounds with the customers, I could see Judy in a back booth rubbing at her nose, studying the menu like a legal document, probably telling those stray friends what a son of a bitch her father was, and that they should order the most expensive item on the menu. They usually did; she mostly settled for a club sandwich.

Jean's diction isn't really out of keeping with the way he normally talks. He uses down to earth phrases like "son of a bitch." But he is also able to analyze the complexity of her feelings toward him, and to convey his self-awareness about how she perceives him. He is both the object of those emotions, and a commentator on them. He doesn't blame her for her negative feelings; if anything, he blames himself. At the same time, he seems to be giving his side of the story, letting us know that in his own way, he was trying to keep an eye on her during that difficult time for both of them. Usually, this kind of multi-layered tone gets reserved for the third person, where an "outside" narrator, real or implied, is telling the story. As you can see, however, the use of voice allows first-person narration to be just as open as third person.

In both of the above passages, Jean asks for forgiveness and absolution from a family member. But he has to use different parts of the same voice for that task. In the first case, a heavier reliance on country dialect is in order. It wouldn't do at all to

say, in the second passage, that his daughter Judy was "hankering" after the free restaurant food. It's much more logical and
appropriate, in her case, to simply say that she wanted it. And
yet, both "wanted" and "hankered" can be part of the same
character's dialect, as long as that dialect remains rooted in the
more encompassing notion of voice. The cardinal sin that a
writer can commit, in my opinion, is being condescending to
his or her characters. Learning how to control the element of
voice allows you to use dialect without condescension.

PRESERVING THE INFLECTIONS OF THE INDIVIDUAL VOICE

A second example of the way voice and dialect work together
and enhance each other comes from another chapter of the
same novel, *Kentuckiana*, when Jean's wife, Constance, speaks
about her conflicts with a different daughter in the family,
named Talia. Even though Constance grew up only a few miles
away from Jean, her social ambitions, and the way she thinks
about her relationship to her small-town past is quite different
from his, and therefore her dialect cannot be the same as his.
If anything, she wants to lose the way of talking she was raised
into, and make something different out of herself.

Like Jean, she tells her part of the story in first person, and
like him, she does have a dialect. Except that her "dialect" is
marked not by country speech, but more by syntax, the way she
strings her sentences together. Her logic is associative, meaning
that her thoughts jump ceaselessly from one subject to another
as she frets over the problems of her various children, trying
not to play favorites. The comic effect of her voice depends on
having the reader, rather than Constance herself, become
aware of how casually she tosses off descriptive hand grenades
about her children's idiosyncrasies.

>   That particular Christmas was a little strange all
> around. It had been a hard year for Stephen, and he was
> in a therapy called co-counseling, where you and your

friends go into a room together and laugh and cry a lot. Also he was in the middle of rehearsals for a play in French or Spanish, or was it Portugese, and while I basted the turkey with an eyedropper, I could hear him in the bedroom above me by himself, shouting out these speeches in a foreign language, like somebody speaking in tongues. Elaine was the only one who had her act together enough to help me cook, make the dumplings and oysters and so forth. Judy had flown back from the southwest on a midnight cargo flight, and she stayed at the attic Talia was renting because as it turned out they were both into black men and discotheques that year—well, Talia was at least, and Judy curious, on the rebound after her divorce.

There's nothing out of the ordinary about Constance's way of speaking: no funny spellings, no half-understood vocabulary that might require a glossary. If anything, the words she uses at first sound perilously close to Standard American English. But the more she talks, the more one realizes there is certainly nothing standard about the content of what Constance says, nor in the way she says it. She has a habit of cramming as much devastating information as she can into a single paragraph, always in a rush to get the facts out of her mouth so she can try to make sense of them. This particular cadence of speech is as much a "dialect" as the archaisms that issue from the mouths of James Still's characters. The secret is out: Suburbanites have accents too. And a character like Constance, hanging on to the middle class by one fingernail, trying not to fall back into poverty, has every reason to try (without success) to erase the telltale marks of her small-town upbringing from her speech.

If a definition of dialect can be given at this point, one might say that dialect marks out the relation between an individual character and his or her regional setting. The reason a lot of people have trouble with dialect is that they focus too much on the relation between the region and the rest of the country. They would get much better results by focusing on the relation of the individual to the other inhabitants of his or her region. Jean and Constance's son, Stephen, in *Kentuckiana*, is probably at the largest remove of all the novel's characters from his Kentucky upbringing. He is the one least directly affected by the speech habits of his kin, and most aware of the fact that he has modified those habits of speech. The further away he moves, the more acutely aware he becomes of the distance separating him from his origins.

BALANCING AND UNBALANCING DIALECT AND VOICE

In Stephen's portions of the novel, he uses what the Nebraska novelist Wright Morris would call "gentle self-mockery" to puzzle out the relation between himself and his family. He doesn't want to be different, but he is. In fact, his family requires of him that he be different. This state of affairs makes the authorial voice much stronger in Stephen's story than it is in other parts of the novel, and tilts the equation between dialect and voice much more strongly toward voice. In one of Stephen's chapters, "The Wunderkind," he playfully makes fun of himself because in junior high, while learning elementary French, he used his budding foreign language and the fact that his impoverished family insisted on thinking of him as a "child genius," as a way of accentuating the troublesome difference between himself and them.

The use of irony through voice allows Stephen to realize, at a much later age, how that precocious child was, at the same time, both a snob and a vulnerable little boy. The technique voice provides (an older self commenting on a younger one) also allows him to mock his snobbery, and invite the reader to do the same—but, without making him give up the affection that he still feels toward the childlike self of those bygone days. Without the flexibility of voice, the character would doubtless end up sounding either too nostalgic or too arch. As it is, the writer can have it both ways. The voice allows us to laugh at the absurdity of a twelve year old putting on airs, but points to Stephen's somewhat painful awareness that in a way, his family saw his intelligence in dead serious as their salvation.

I punished on occasion my own family's inattention to my workings by such means as making incomprehensible remarks at the table. After a supper of fried salmon croquettes and rehydrated au gratin potatoes, when we sat together in a rare moment of satiated silence, I would turn to my mother and in a French rendered perfect by the brevity of my question, I'd ask, *"Et alors?"* with a look of expectancy, as if we were a Tolstoyan family of princes and princesses accustomed to switching casually back and forth between our native tongue and French as we planned our after-dinner sleigh ride through the *bois.*

Stephen knows full well that his modest family has nothing whatsoever to do with princes and princesses out of Tolstoy. The only rich thing about them is their fantasy life, and his remarkable intelligence allows them, in turn, to dream great dreams about what might be possible in the midst of poverty. Because he is the child philosopher, pure of heart, he is allowed the biggest vocabulary and the most complex sentences. Those things weigh on him like a badge of honor, so heavy, so awkward and so gaudy that the hero is a little bit embarrassed to be wearing it.

The labyrinthine twistings and turnings of his mind, in this sense, beg to be called a dialect. They make up the net of words he is enmeshed in, whether he likes it or not. He speaks at times almost with the studied formality one might expect of a medieval knight-errant. At the same time, his self-effacing wit and his sly sense of humor work to undercut the complexity of his language. The gravest sin in his father's Appalachian culture is to get above your raising, and Stephen doesn't get above his raising. Stephen's greatest worry is that he will truly become estranged from his clan, and from their characteristic way of putting things.

The success of his peculiar dialect depends almost entirely on the use of voice to mediate between Stephen's sophisticated lingo and the reader. The voice brings out the simplicity of Stephen's heart, otherwise his way of talking could become just as murky and hard to understand as a dialect loaded down with country words like "Nay-o" and "Gee-o" and "Weaky" could be. The thing that makes words hard for a reader to understand, whether they're hillbilly dialect or the polysyllables of a polyglot, is not having a good context for interpreting them. Big words are not frightening in themselves. It is, rather, the wrong words in the wrong places. And voice, above all, is the element of fiction able to put things in the proper context.

The authorial voice clues one in to the essential sweetness of Stephen's character, and to the fact that no matter what he talks about, he is always, at bottom, trying to figure out his family members and express his love for them. The kind of language Stephen uses puts him at the other end of the spectrum from his father's earthy phrases and clipped sentences, or from his mother's rapid-fire plain talk. If Jean is a folk tale, and Constance a self-help manual, then Stephen is a dictionary of nautical terms that somebody has plucked off the dusty shelves of a used bookstore and bought for seventy-five cents. But, strangely, they all belong not only in the same section of the same bookstore, but also on the same shelf, propping each other up.

One is able to gauge how far one generation's speech habits have gone from the previous one's, but also appreciate the affection that exists between them, in one story of *Kentuckiana* when Stephen goes along with his father to sell vacuum cleaners door to door along the rural routes. Stephen comes away impressed by Jean's ability to make a vacuum cleaner sale to a hard-headed farmer, all because Jean knows, like the back of his hand, the psychology and the lingo of rural Kentuckians. Stephen's and Jean's dialects couldn't be more different, but the authorial voice controlling them is one and the same.

THE MECHANICS OF STYLE

One aspect of authorial control that must always be addressed is that of the mechanics of style. A fiction writer's goal, whether you are writing in dialect or more toward the hypothetical voice of Standard American English, is to draw the reader along in such a way that she never stops to question what you're doing with voice. For the reader, that question should never arise, which means that you, the writer, must take care to attend to mechanics beforehand. Like the buffet waiter, you have to arrive at the restaurant three hours beforehand to set up the steam tables so that when you, the silent pair of hands, proffer the plate to the customer, he'll think to himself, like a total ingrate, "This job is a piece of cake. I wish I had such easy work." If you make your reader into an ingrate, in the sense of belying the arduous care with mechanics that has gone into your flawless style, you will have succeeded.

Especially when your grammar is trickiest and most heterodox, you want to make it look like a cinch. If the writer's sense of mechanics remains sure and natural, the reader will accept many grammatical sleights of hand, including dialect liberties, that depart from the conventions of written English language. In speaking of mechanics, and in spite of my blue-collar metaphor, I want to disavow any attempt to evoke the image of a man in an oil-spotted workshirt (the one who really does have a blue collar) sliding under the chassis of your story and loosening the universal joint just before you take your vehicle out for a high-speed romp on the highway. If there is a mechanic present in these pages, he is more like my Albuquerque friend, the one who dreams of math while tinkering with carburetors, understanding mathematics as quite possibly an exact science, but more likely an ethereal one.

Fiction criticism, by its nature, remains more impressionistic than the kind of rhetoric that can be applied, say, to formal poetry. Metrics, prosody, couplets, scansion, enjambment—these terms, which can be discussed with such measured exactitude in the context of a sonnet, begin to lose their explanatory power within the labyrinth of a novel, or even in the relative containment of a short story. The rough equivalents of these terms do exist within prose fiction—structure, plot, vignette, cadence—but not with anything approaching the strict precision of poetic terms as far as mechanics and rhetoric are concerned. In speaking of some of those critical terms already, I've tried to take them as far as their relevance allows without pretending that they constitute a taxonomical catalog worthy of a zoologist at the museum of natural history.

To be sure, commentators on fiction have made arduous, even heroic attempts to give the analysis of style and mechanics a scientistic luster, bringing over sometimes wholesale, sometimes with modifications, fuel injectors, bored-out pistons and baffling butterfly baffles—in short, the terminology of standard grammar and rhetoric. But souped-up rhetorical figures can only take us so far in the understanding of style. Anacoluthons, though they do exist, sometimes in abundance, sound more likely to inhabit a literary bestiary by Julio Cortázar or Jorge Luis Borges than they do one of our sentences.

Learning to identify an anacoluthon—defined by rhetoricians as "an abrupt change within a sentence to a second grammatical construction inconsistent with the first"—may in fact not even end up improving our grammar, much less our style. Therefore, let us not be too eager to hunt each one down until the anacoluthon appears on the list of endangered grammatical species. Besides, there's nothing whatsoever wrong with an abrupt change in grammatical construction, when it's used for a deliberate rhetorical effect. If I mix my metaphors in midstream, or switch my horses while they're drinking water, or lure my anacoluthon to a salt lick, I simply have to ask myself first whether I have a justifiable reason for doing so.

This is not to undervalue the importance of grammar to graceful prose, of stylistics to style, or to say that voice should be invoked as a disclaimer for shoddy sentence construction. In fiction, there are no excuses. Every page of every story becomes an execution of method, and as such gets judged as either foolproof or foolscap. At the moment of reading, we all become executioners, who permit no stays of execution. Yet it wouldn't do to speak of grammar as having "laws," in quite the same way we speak of "the laws of physics."

Besides, speaking of laws makes it sound as though grammar muzzles a writer, or puts her in a straitjacket if she doesn't obey its dictatorial dictates. No matter how merciless the requirements of style, we shouldn't conceive of our relation to grammar as punitive. Language does have its rules, yet even they are more a matter of decorum than of legality. What separates decorum from the law is that we adhere to it on a voluntary basis, and the definition of what can be permitted as proper changes depending on the company you're keeping.

Cussing a Blue Streak

Let's take the example of obscenity. It's not a bad example, considering how obscenity has proliferated in modern writing, to the point that many writers don't seem to give a f _ _ _ one way or the other. The David Mamets of theater and the Jay McInerneys of fiction might tend to ask me what the big f _ _ _ ing deal is, who the f _ _ _ am I to make an issue of obscenity. And in a sense, they're right. On the other hand, there are discriminations to be made.

As with any point of style, there exists an upper limit beyond which you start to reap diminishing returns, on account of stylistic overkill. In my view, Mamet's best work (*American Buffalo* and *Glengarry Glen Ross*), walks this line successfully, creating what I refer to as "the poetry of poverty." That is, the power of his characters derives from their struggle to express meaningful statements about their degraded human condition using the most meager materials possible. Passion and a longing for language undergird their inarticulate epithets.

David Rabe does something similar in his ferocious play *Sticks and Bones*. Jay McInerney and Brett Easton Ellis, on the other hand, seem to wallow so much in the shock value of obscenity that they lose view of the fact that, like all the other language in a novel, cursing is a stylistic resource. As in the case of dialect, too much cursing tends to create a more watered down version than using none at all would.

The rightness or wrongness of using an obscenity is defined not so much by the expression itself as by the context in which it is used. As the speaker or writer, you're simply enjoined to consider beforehand what the likely effect of your utterance will be, and then, having weighed the possible consequences, you decide whether or not you're going to go ahead and utter it. I can cite the word "shit" as one such example, and get away with it in the context of this grammatical excursus on obscenity. Besides, I've loaded the deck by throwing in the word "excursus" at the end of the last sentence—in hopes that while you're wavering between looking up "excursus" in the dictionary, and deciding that it probably just has something to do with the word "curse," and it isn't worth the trouble of rooting around for the dictionary, you'll maybe forget that I even used the word "shit" in the first place.

Even if you don't forget, you may decide that the quotation marks around the word in the above sentence distance me enough from the offensive term that you'll absolve me from any direct responsibility for its use. He's not relishing the word, you'll say to yourself, he's only citing it. However, if I were to then go on for several paragraphs berating you for being a shitty writer, you might not feel so forgiving. You'd take it personally. The emphasis and heat with which I spoke the epithet, or the careless, colloquial familiarity I lent it, make me responsible for its use in a different way. It's all a matter of context.

This example can serve to sketch out a working definition of a fiction writer's flexible relationship to general questions of mechanics, usage and grammar in fiction. Too many beginning writers are eager to break the rules before they even understand what those rules might be and why they don't like them. Don't let a reflex rebelliousness against rules lead you to reject them just on principle, regardless of their particular content. Depressingly, even slang—especially slang—has predictable features.

Rules of grammar exist simply to provide us with a shared understanding of what the possibilities of our language are. With them, we can gauge how much flexibility the language is ready to grant us before we begin to do it violence. In any point of usage, we have to know where the breaking point lies. That way, at least we know where convention leaves off and the real testing begins. For that reason, following the cue of George Levine, I advocate the idea of formulating mechanics to ourselves in the form of an "if-then" proposition.

If we want to achieve such-and-such an effect, *then* we have to follow a certain set of guidelines. The guidelines will vary depending on what effect we wish to produce at any given time. This approach puts more emphasis on descriptive formulations than it does on prescriptive formulas. I'm using the word now in the sense that we speak of "descriptive linguistics" and "descriptive anthropology." (This should not be confused with my distinction, in chapter eight, between the descriptive and discursive voices. I mean the word "descriptive" here only in the restricted sense I've just mentioned.)

You look at a piece of writing—someone else's or your own—and you start figuring out what it is that you've wrought, and why certain parts of it seem lackluster and others vibrant. Some are humming, others barely chug along. You pay close attention to the inner workings of your prose, but you don't hasten to bring in the "mechanics" who want to rush under the hood and start tinkering and cootering right off.

In critiquing my students, I might focus on one or two general notions about grammar, but I try to formulate these concerns in the larger context of what I feel they are trying to accomplish in a given story. As Isaac Babel instructs us, a writer doesn't adhere to grammar out of "dead scholasticism," but rather out of a living engagement with the materials of fiction.

Exercises

1. Write a page of regional dialogue between two characters. First, use phonetic spellings, to try to reproduce as closely as possible the sense of how you think the characters would actually sound. This will be the "transcription" version. Now try rewriting that same dialogue, only this time using just a few selected words or phrases that you think represent the way those characters would speak. Write with normal spellings, without using apostrophes at the ends of words, etc. Concentrate as much on the syntax—the order of words and arrangement of phrases and clauses—as you do on the words themselves. Strive to put the right words in the right place. This will be the "representation" version of the dialogue. Compare the two to see what you have been able to achieve in each version, and to discover which one comes closer to communicating the essence of the character types you want to portray.

2. Spend a few minutes sitting in a public place, writing down, as exactly as you can, an open conversation that two people are having. It doesn't really matter what the conversation is about, or whether it seems at the time banal or interesting to you. Make sure, if possible, that you write several pages of dialogue, to have as much to work with as possible. Take this transcript home and rewrite the dialogue into a dramatized scene. You should feel free to change the content of the conversation as much as suits your purposes. You'll find in any case that you have to make changes, if the conversation is to be compelling as *fiction*, because people's actual conversations tend to be less interesting, word for word, than the ones you find in good books. What is equally important, however, is that you preserve in your rewrite the particular flavor of how each person speaks. You will probably discover that as you try to capture the essence of their speech for your fictional needs, you will be forced to stylize it. This should make you much more aware of how selection of what is *representative* about people's speech is the key to successful dialect.

3. Think of a person you know reasonably well, but who is as different from you as possible, in terms of class, region, manner of dress, body language and personal habits. Write a two-page vignette in which you report conversations you have had over time with that person, using actual quotes, reproduced from memory, of things that person has said. Based on these quotes, give an interpretation of your friendship with that person, including his or her faults and good points, and what makes that person interesting to you. You are the narrator, and that person is a character in your tale, in effect. Now perform the same exercise, reversing the roles. Make the person you know into the first-person narrator of the "report," and yourself the object whose quotes are being used as "material." Imagine what that person might have to say about you as a friend or colleague. Performing this third exercise should begin to make you aware of how the voice of the narrator shapes the voice of the character. Both voices have color, and each depends on the other for success.

CHAPTER 6

DEFINING
THE SUBJECT

THE MOST ANXIOUS TIME OF COMPOSITION tends to be the beginning of a project, when the writer faces a blank screen or paper. This feeling of uneasiness can sometimes carry over into each day of writing, multiplying itself like bad copies struck from a defective master, so that the prospect of getting going every morning in a fresh state of mind begins to seem insurmountably difficult. In his book *Twenty Lines a Day*, Harry Mathews describes his preferred means of getting around that dilemma.

> Like many writers, I often find starting the working day a discouraging prospect, one that I spend much energy avoiding. Four years ago I was reminded of an injunction Stendahl gave himself early in life: Twenty lines a day, genius or not. Stendahl was thinking about getting a book done. I deliberately mistook his words as a method for overcoming the anxiety of the blank page.

Mathews's method of using the twenty lines as an entity unto itself is praiseworthy, because he spends a certain, guaranteed amount of time each day thinking small, working on finger exercises that will presumably, over the long haul, warm him up for bigger and more daunting projects. Stendahl, on the other hand, invites us to punch the clock daily, holding ourselves to a minimum standard of quantity, without worrying too much about quality. Quality, he assumes, will take care of itself if you set yourself up with your instruments of creation.

The poet Jim Wayne Miller once commented, "If you're suffering from writer's block, lower your standards. If you're still suffering from writer's block, lower your standards some more." The crucial thing is to set up circumstances such that you write, rather than spend your time thinking of reasons why you can't write. Either of these paths, Stendahl's or Mathews's, is a good point of departure. They teach a form of self-discipline, which becomes the successful writer's most important quality. A writer is, quite simply, one who writes.

Still, these paths don't necessarily lead one to a way of sustaining a larger project, a vision of the artifact, whether that artifact be a short story, a novella or a novel. Twenty lines a day is a good way to begin, but those hundreds or thousands of lines, over time, may or may not add up to a whole and accomplished work of fiction. In the absence of any larger vision, they probably won't. You'll end up instead with reams of jottings, and will find that you're writing toward a beginning, waiting for it to reveal itself. The root of writer's block can usually be traced back to the deceptively simple question, What do I want to write about? And any solution, therefore, must help the writer define the subject.

To do so, you will need recourse to the story's primary voice. Subjects do not arise in a vacuum. Teresa Porzecanski told me once in an interview that her stories usually begin with a voice speaking a phrase that she can't get out of her head. Even those writers who tend to begin with an image will find that one image soon leads to another, and before you know it you have a concatenation of images. In order for those images to have a secure and credible connection to one another, they will need to be animated by voice. That's why we say "a train of thought": The objects of thought must be set in motion, and voice provides that motion.

RUMMAGING THROUGH THE BASEMENT

Defining the subject, on the face of it, seems like it ought to be the easiest of tasks. Even if you don't keep a notebook or a journal, you most likely have stored inside your mind a set of notions, something like those cardboard boxes of memorabilia from childhood, and gifts, toys and utensils from adulthood that you've hauled around from state to state, apartment to apartment, house to house, without ever getting rid of completely. Once in a while, in a fit of determination, you resolve to yourself, "I'm either going to find a use for this junk, or trash it." Then you pluck out one or two objects, maybe the fondue set your sister gave you at your wedding, telling you that it would provide you with a whole different perspective on tofu. Or maybe the bright orange, ten-foot hammock you bought in the Yucatan, and saved for the time when you would finally live in a place with stout, shady trees in the backyard.

And although you still don't like tofu, and you still can't figure out where they sell those little cans of sterno, you decide to use the fondue pot as a serving dish, and let people spear their cubes of pepper jack cheese with miniature harpoons. You screw one end of the hammock into the garage and the other into a telephone pole. Then you screw up your courage to throw out some of the precious but unusable bric-a-brac you've held onto for the biblical seven years. You make a little space to acquire and store a few more notions. But whatever happens, you'll never get rid of those cardboard boxes, and they will always stay full, because they're part of you. In an odd way, they define you. They're valuable, even if only you know their true value. But if you're a writer, you've got to figure out a way to convince other people of their value.

Most writers have sufficient life experience, have read a fair amount, and have plenty of ideas, in various states of coherence and incoherence, hopping about in their heads. Unfortunately, they're not always visions of sugarplums. The mind can be crowded with images, scenes, bits of dialogue and place names, but without providing you with any clue about how to sort out which of these is the speck of unburnished gold amid the lode of silt. A friend of mine described a rather strange car ride he once took through rural Idaho with his aunt. As he stared out at the ore-colored hills, the journey seemed long to him, first of all, because the aunt chattered on incessantly. But the amount of talking didn't bother him so much as the fact that it all seemed to come out in a single, undifferentiated rush. There was no quality control. She couldn't sort out the things she was saying in terms of establishing which was more or less important than the other. All of them existed, to her mind, on an equal plane.

"These pretzels are my favorite kind because they're mustard flavored and not so salty by the way your second cousin Duane is very sick they say he might not make it did you know him? I can't understand why you decided to go to college on the West Coast there's just no weather out there I wish Bill would change the tires on our car they're way too slick and we could have a blowout at any moment I wonder if he took those coupons with him to the store, probably not. This man at his work is going through the awfulest divorce, they served the papers on him last month."

Although his aunt would make for an interesting and eccentric character in a story, she wouldn't be a very good author, because there's no sense of setting priorities, or of realizing which of her sundry, sordid, banal topics might hold the nephew's interest for longer than an instant. The constant shifts in topic indicate that she herself probably doesn't have much faith that anything she's saying is, in the end, of much interest to anybody. The problem, at bottom, is usually not a lack of something to say, or the lack of a subject about which to write. You know what your tastes and passions run to, but you don't always know how to articulate the essence of what is interesting about them to someone else. Overcoming writer's block begins with the realization that there are, strictly speaking, no fresh subjects available to you. You need not sit at the computer waiting for the truly fascinating and unique subject to present itself to you, like the angel of annunciation showing itself to Mary. As I have said, subject cannot divorce itself for long from an animating voice, and as often as not, voice will precede subject. If you find yourself discarding topic after topic, that's a strong indicator, not that your ideas are dead on arrival, but that voice needs to be breathed into one of them. If I were going to obey Stendahl's and Mathews's injunctions about twenty lines a day, I would devote my twenty lines to discovering the story's primary voice.

LETTING THE PRIMARY VOICE SPEAK

Once you have established the story's voice, whether it be the narrator of a story or its principal character speaking through dialogue and reflection, the other elements will begin to build themselves around it. When you begin writing fiction, and in particular a novel, you may automatically use as your protagonist the first character who suggests itself to your mind. Before long, other characters will start to present themselves as well, to whom the protagonist will exist in relation—neighbors, friends, enemies, a lover, a family.

But perhaps one of these "secondary" characters could possess the primary voice you're after. Try composing passages in several of the character voices, giving each the chance to become the narrator. In theater, the purpose of an audition is to give the various contestants a chance to vie for the roles of the principals, rather than assuming beforehand which will be suitable for which. Even in terms of point of view, it is advisable to keep an open mind at the outset. In a first person narration, the protagonist does not have to be the narrator. Think how differently Fitzgerald's *The Great Gatsby* would read if it had been told by Gatsby himself, rather than his neighbor Nick Carroway. In that instance, a secondary character narrates the entire novel, becoming the primary voice, and it was obviously the right choice.

Other times, the character may be only one of the principals within the novel, yet serve as its primary voice. When Vladimir Nabokov found the right narrator for *Lolita*, it was a pretty good bet that the novel would find an interesting shape. Humbert Humbert, the narrator, is not the title character. He has been taken into legal custody for murder, and begins to recount the story of his love and lust for the nymphet Lolita. Nabokov knows that the reader is apt from the outset to want to judge Humbert harshly, not only for killing a man, but even more for his supposed seduction and corrupting of a female minor.

But Nabokov has ideas of his own. Aware that we're not predisposed to let Humbert off the hook, he's determined not to let us off the hook either—especially not off the narrative hook. If we're not going to show any mercy, neither will he. He's schooled in the psychology of the kind of person who would stand in the supermarket line, reading the front page of the *National Enquirer*, rationalizing to himself that since he's not paying for it, and since he's just waiting to have his groceries scanned, it doesn't really count if he does some scanning of his own. Nabokov knows that deep down, inquiring minds want to know. So he provides, for our inquiring minds, not a Humbert remorseful or ashamed, but one who, on the contrary, is ready to tell us, in detail, all about how he developed a yen for a barely pubescent girl with a mind of her own. Humbert, the narrator, would rather recount his sins than recant them.

> Lolita, light of my life, fire of my loins. My sin, my soul. Lo-lee-ta: the tip of the tongue taking a trip of three steps down the palate to tap, at three, on the teeth. Lo. Lee. Ta.
> Did she have a precursor? She did, indeed she did. In point of fact, there might have been no Lolita at all had I not loved, one summer, a certain initial girl-child. In a princedom by the sea. Oh when? About as many years before Lolita was born as my age was that summer. You can always count on a murderer for a fancy prose style.
> Ladies and gentlemen of the jury, exhibit number one is what the seraphs, the misinformed, simple, noble-winged seraphs, envied. Look at this tangle of thorns.

The voice establishes itself in a few choice sentences. We know that, throughout the tale, Humbert is going to be witty, charming, entertaining. We know that we're going to get our money's worth. The confession is going to be juicy. It will titillate us much more than those stories about Elvis's love-child, which always sound so appealing on the tabloid cover, and always disappoint us when we get to the back pages of the *Enquirer* and find out that after all it's only a sketchy news item based on something supposedly said by a friend of Priscilla Presley's in the waiting room of the Thai nail salon.

Humbert, on the other hand, is going to give us all the gory details, just as promised. He may be rueful, but he's not ashamed, and so he will tell all, including the sex. Most especially the sex. Or at least we hope so—not that we usually go for that sort of thing. Still, we are going to have to pay a price for getting this inside glimpse. Just when we're about to sneer that the dirty old man who despoiled *Lolita* is going to try to get himself off the hook by protesting the innocence of his romantic feelings—"a princedom by the sea"—he reminds us that we're in the position of judging his actions. And if we're supposed to have the moral upper hand, then we can't very well get too involved in the lurid details. Otherwise, we'll be like those hypocritical men on the board of censors who screen the pornographic film in a private room—several times—before pronouncing it unfit for public consumption.

Humbert tweaks us, and himself, by commenting that "You can always count on a murderer for a fancy prose style." Have we already convicted him in our hearts? Is he guilty until proven innocent? If so, then we must spare ourselves the indignity of reading any further, because he has no intention of trying to convince us of his innocence. On the contrary, he's going to smart off, make puns and jokes, some of them at our expense. He's going to revel in his sin, wallow in it, make fun of America and its Puritanism. Naturally, we hurry on to the next paragraph, to see what other prose tricks he has up his sleeve. But not before he reminds us that we are "Ladies and gentlemen of the jury." Impertinent man that he is, he accuses us (unjustly!) of thinking badly of him and his lust because we secretly envy him his nubile corruptor of seraphs. Of all the nerve!

The narrating voice is in firm control of the story before it divulges any of the particulars. It's not only sin, but style, that seduces us. The deck is pleasantly stacked against the reader. Nabokov has made a good decision in choosing, for this tale, a first-person narrator who is suave, well-educated, and as pithy as a Granny Smith apple. Nabokov, a natural wordsmith, plays to his own strengths by endowing his narrator with a silver tongue. The reader dares Humbert to talk his way out of this one, and Humbert does. Or at the least, he talks us into where he is, deep into his obsession with *Lolita*.

KEEPING CONTROL OF THE EXPANSIVE VOICE

Zora Neale Hurston takes another tack altogether. In *Their Eyes Were Watching God*, she wants to tell the individual story of an earthy woman, Janie Crawford, awakening to herself in a little Florida town. At the same time, she wishes to relate the story of the community in which Janie lives. It's a place where, in most respects, your business is everybody's business, and so, appropriately, Hurston selects a third-person narrator, although attention remains on Janie as the focal character—what Henry James calls a "center of consciousness." Strictly speaking, this technique is anchored in point of view. However, point of view in a restricted sense can't account fully for the narrator's qualities. There are many types of third-person narrators, and their qualities of voice can differ greatly from one another. The third-person narrator is anything but neutral. One may not be able to describe the narrator with certainty as a he or a she, but it is decidedly not an "it."

This type of narrator weds the sensibility of the author with that of an unnamed character who participates and/or comments on events in the story while remaining close to the action or remote from it to varying degrees. In *Their Eyes Were Watching God*, Hurston establishes in the first paragraphs an expansive voice capable of embracing the sensibility of the entire community. A big narrator like this must be kept in tight control. The voice is both mired in the community members' passions, and hovers above them, commenting and making known general truths about the human condition. Hurston's very first sentence states a law of life that sounds more than anything like a proverb: "Ships at a distance have every man's wish onboard." Proverbs may seem incompatible with modern fiction, because they express themselves in the language of global thoughts: "every man's wish." But the most revered modern authors, from Tolstoy and Joyce to Ralph Ellison and Hurston, have borrowed heavily from folk sources, including proverbs. The challenge is to use these sources without letting your fiction become proverbial.

The voice in *Their Eyes Were Watching God* avoids this pitfall by skillfully walking the line between the particular and the general. It goes on to explain the meaning of the proverb, and concludes its initial thought by stating "That is the life of men." But before long, the narrator has turned to the specific case of Janie, still without giving us her name. Instead, she is a woman, everywoman. She could be any woman who has had to go through the melancholy experience of putting her man in a cold hole in the ground.

> So the beginning of this was a woman and she had come back from burying the dead. Not the dead of sick and ailing with friends at the pillow and the feet. She had come back from the sudden and the bloated; the sudden dead, their eyes flung wide open in judgement.

In this novel, everyone, even the dead, has eyes to see and a mouth with which to tell a tale. It's said that dead men don't tell tales, but this is not the case in Hurston's world, where traditions spread themselves over the countryside like pollen. Even as the narrator, in a voice tinged with compassion, homes in on Janie's personal existence, it's clear that this is not going to be a personal confession like Humbert's. Personal grief remains bound up with communal life, so that Janie's deceased husband gets classified as one of the two types of dead: the "sudden" ones, "their eyes flung wide open in judgement."

The novel defines him not only by how he meets his end, but by how he is or isn't mourned by the people around him. His existence belongs to them as much as it does to him. The voice Hurston employs for this task of describing rituals could easily be that of a member of this community. Just as the story doesn't ask the reader to ponder the name of the dead man, it doesn't really matter exactly who the voice's identity is. He or she is a part of the flow and pulse of life, and Hurston uses the voice in a way that allows it to extract the juice from the situation, offering up to us what is elemental, an essence.

MANY VOICES SPEAKING AS ONE

Hurston offers a different kind of sophistication from Nabo-kov's. Instead of a tightly controlled individual voice all over the map with its plays on words, allusions and hundred dollar vocabulary, Hurston uses a broader voice that encompasses more, but with a deliberate simplicity; without contradiction, both shallow and deep. This voice is just as distinctive as Hum-bert's, without possessing the same pedigree. It doesn't mean to wow us and throw us off balance with its self-mocking "fancy prose style." The impression it leaves is bold, forceful, indelible, like a woodcut. It speaks from the patience that springs from enduring through eons. It gathers many voices into one, but without becoming vague or losing the sharpness that one tends to associate with individual characters.

> The people all saw her come because it was sundown. The sun was gone, but he had left his footprints in the sky. It was the time for sitting on porches beside the road. It was the time to hear things and talk. These sitters had been tongueless, earless, eyeless conveniences all day long. Mules and other brutes had occupied their skin. But now, the sun and the bossman were gone, so the skins felt pow-erful and human. They became lords of sounds and lesser things. They passed nations through their mouths. They sat in judgement.

In *Their Eyes Were Watching God*, the characters, and not we the readers, stand in judgement. With the progression toward eve-ning, in the twilight hour, this community of blacks who have had to sweat out their labor through the workday, start to re-cover their humanity. For a few brief hours, they are refreshed, done with "mules and other brutes." One of the advantages of this type of voice is that it allows Hurston to elevate the diction when she needs to, so that it sounds almost biblical, but without becoming pretentious. It's hard to say "They passed nations through their mouths" with a straight face. Try it, and you'll see. Yet this narrator pulls it off. Unlike Humbert, she gets away with murder. Or is she a he? The murderer's identity remains a mystery, but her voice is, all the same, sharp and clear. The cadences sound soft, and Hurston has already established its authority to be both lofty and down to earth. Humble people, in the cool of a shaded porch in the evening, can fancy themselves lords.

Like all humans, these characters can act in a manner less than noble. They use their princely power, not to ponder great moral questions, but petty ones. They prefer to sit in judgement by gossiping about Janie, who is returning from the task of burying her husband. They are, after all, lords of "lesser things." This capacious voice, with the slightest change in inflection, injects some irony into the situation. The pronouncements are large, but the method is subtle. It gradually comes down to where we reside, so to speak, at street level, sitting on the porches with the scoffing townspeople. Hurston hasn't allowed the watcher's gaze to settle into any single pair of eyes. All their eyes are watching God, and watching Janie. Like the eyes of the drowned husband, they accuse, but for different reasons. They don't approve of a forty-year-old woman who went off and married a younger man. In their opinion, she has gotten her just deserts.

> Seeing the woman as she was made them remember the envy they had stored up from other times. So they chewed up the back parts of their minds and swallowed with relish. They made burning statements with questions, and killing tools out of laughs. It was mass cruelty. A mood come alive. Words walking without masters; walking altogether like harmony in a song.

Note that while the narrating voice sounds harshly critical of the jeering watchers, accusing them of "mass cruelty," the voice also is appreciative of the townspeople's vitality, even when that vitality expresses itself as hatred and envy. It is "altogether like harmony in a song." When a mood comes alive, its sheer energy will carry the moment, regardless of its content. Passion is a form of excess, usually destructive, but also the

index of life. This voice forgives the townspeople in advance
for the accusation it plans to make against them. In the end,
the narrator, too, is concerned with lesser things. It begins with
its eyes looking down from above, and ends gazing up at heaven
from below. Because it becomes so intermingled with the characters it is describing, the voice knows well enough not to hand
down the law to its tribe on stone tablets. That kind of arro-
gance, in Hurston's world, usually gets punished.

Hurston was trained as a folklorist, and spent time collect-
ing folk tales throughout the South, so she cultivated a respect
for the voice of folk wisdom. While employing techniques of
modern fiction, she knew that she couldn't truly improve upon
that folk voice. Therefore, she made the narrator's voice an
outgrowth of the folk voice. It's a fair bet that the subject didn't
come to Hurston first. Instead, she heard a lilt, a cadence, whis-
pering like the Devil at her ear. And that devilish voice contained the story that would then become the apple of her eye.

Like her, if a voice suggests itself to you strongly enough,
learn to respect it, rather than immediately feeling you have to
improve on it, tame it, subordinate it. It is something of a romantic notion to believe that art is dictated to us by outside
"voices." But in a limited and more realistic sense, you can
attune your ear to listening carefully when the primary voice
begins to speak. Begin by cultivating an awareness of the conversations going on around you every day. They are the stuff
of fiction. Some will strike you as throwaways, others as keepers.

TEACHING AN OLD DOG NEW TRICKS

Sometimes, the subject of the story presents itself to the mind
less as a definite idea than as a problem to be solved. Say you
want to tell a love story about a couple, twenty-something,
maybe thirty-something, who don't communicate very well. The
contours of this would-be story aren't as sharp as you'd like
them to be. He's into watching sports, and can't open up about
himself. She wants to talk about the relationship. It's an old
story, love. One that's been done before, to say the least. And

the wrinkle of men and TV sports—well, that one's been kicked around as well, like a weekend warrior's football that, like him, has seen better days. The stand-up comics have done the topic to death. An urban anthropologist could collect three dozen versions of the urban viking in a single night by sitting on a stool in a sports bar with a tape recorder.

Then again, maybe that's your story. If it is, the fact that it's been told before shouldn't necessarily keep you from giving your version of it. Shakespeare's plots were not so terribly original, and brazen bard that he was, he didn't care who knew it. He stole most of the ideas for his history plays from a historian named Raphael Holinshed. But who outside of academia has ever heard of Holinshed? Wright Morris was always enchanted by the line in Flaubert's famous story, "A Simple Heart," that describes the servant woman Felicité's memories of her former romantic life in these spare and unsparing words: "She'd had her lover, like another." This sentence, in a single breath, says that: 1) people's amours, because they comprise such a common denominator of human life, are mundane, tedious, not worthy of our interest, and 2) to each person, and each fictional character, his or her amorous life, no matter how tame or done in by the taxidermy of memory, is a cherished and unique possession, the head of the moose, the heart of the artichoke, the stuff of existence.

The challenge is to make that stuff into art. Your best ally in these circumstances, the most reliable Cyrano de Bergerac to pen your inarticulate longings into readable prose, is voice. A story I selected to include in an issue of a literary magazine that I guest-edited had to solve that very question for itself. And it impressed me with its solution. Its skillful understanding of voice led me to pluck it out of a cold submission pile of hundreds of manuscripts, and keep on reading until I got to the end. It spoke to me, as all good stories do. Owen Perkins's "Algebra: A Problem With Words," makes ingenious use of a form familiar to every elementary schoolchild: the math class "word problem."

Or, as they used to cruelly misname it in the grade school I attended, a "story problem." As everyone knows, the textbook story problem is the lowest common denominator of the world of fiction, using the barest elements of story for strictly pedagogical purposes. For instance: "One car is travelling toward Cincinnati at sixty-five miles an hour. A second car, etc. . . ." Nothing could be drier; nothing could disappoint our expectations of a rousing good tale more keenly than the bare-bones generic anecdote about vehicles travelling through empty space at varying speeds, toward cities seemingly devoid of human populations. Why, we ask ourselves, would they want to go to those cities at any speed? I always wanted to cry out to them, "Slow down! Turn back and drive in the other direction before it's too late!" They never heeded my call. The voice of the "narrator" droned on, like that of my earnest math teacher in a room that was too hot, half an hour before recess.

Whimsy With a Straight Face

In "Algebra: A Problem With Words," Owen Perkins cleverly turns the situation to his advantage by playing off our expectation of dryness, and then infusing the voice of his narrator, who is also the central character, with humor, whimsy and regret. Without these qualities of voice, the story could have easily turned into a brittle exercise in technique. Instead, the story's playfulness bubbles up at the beginning, as the forlorn hero starts out to tell a simple word problem, and gets drawn irresistibly and soon into philosophical musings, both silly and profound, that have no answer.

> A man at a station in Baltimore gets on a train traveling at sixty miles an hour headed for New Haven at 10:00 on a Monday morning. Another man at a station in Santa Fe gets on a train traveling seventy miles an hour headed for Colorado Springs at 9:30 Tuesday morning. Will the two trains meet? What time will the two trains meet? What variables will determine when the two trains meet? Who do the two men on the two trains meet? Even if the two trains meet, do the two men on the trains meet each other?

Within a single paragraph, a reader goes from feeling she's

back in math class, to suspecting she's back even further, in the opening passage of a nineteenth century novel. *In the town of _____, on a winter's day in 18____, a young man stood on a train platform waiting for his lady cousin, whom he had never met, to disembark.* Just as in those sprawling novels of Jane Austen and the like, Owen Perkins, through his character's voice, promises that human conflict is going to be involved. It whets my appetite. Even though I know, by strict logic, that the two trains can't meet given their respective destinations, I still hope they will.

In the story's second paragraph, Perkins uses voice to push the whimsy and mild absurdity of the "word problem" even further.

> The man at the station in Baltimore does not carry a guitar. But neither does he carry the New York *Times*. He does carry three papers from Baltimore, the Baltimore *Sun*, the *News American*, and *USA Today*. He buys three papers a day to read the sports section. The dates of the papers are not important. What is important is that the Orioles are winning. The important thing about winning is to win every game.

Suddenly, we find ourselves in the company of a living, breathing being, to be precise, a sports junkie. He has particular tastes, and he likes to win. Still, one has a sneaking suspicion that he isn't going to win at love. As the story proceeds, it becomes evident that the voice telling the story is, or might be, the same as that of one of the characters.

> I am the man on the train from Santa Fe to Colorado Springs. If you happen to know me, you can already tell I'm telling the truth. You can see me sitting in that club car drinking a margarita with an upset stomach from some Mexican food I ate earlier and talking to the bartender. Otherwise, it could be anybody.

Perkins' canny use of this mock-lecturing voice allows the narrator to remain inside and outside the narrative at the same time. He gently makes fun of his own dilemma, his sour stomach and his loneliness, while also maintaining a tone of comic warmth toward the subject. One quality of the voice seems to ask whether all of this, this life business, isn't a little bit trivial after all. Human relationships consist of nothing more or less than a set of equations, and communcation between people boils down to just "a problem with words," as the witty title puts it. The fact that the man likes Mexican food and margaritas is the only thing that feebly differentiates him, in our eyes, from the other passengers on the train. Take those almost generic tastes away, and the character "could be anybody."

At the same time, the speaking voice possesses deep affection for these seemingly trivial affairs. When it says that the character could be anybody, you realize that it could be you, and that if his problems are uninteresting, then so are yours. Indeed, Perkins brings "you" into the story, as the protagonist of one of the most poignant sequences in "Algebra." Some metafictionists, notably John Barth, have used the device of the "you" to browbeat the reader, but Perkins's purposes are quite other. The pretense of anonymity posed by the "word problem" gives way to intimacy. He attempts to establish a bond with the reader through the shared knowledge that talking to people is hard, but that we all want love anyway. You've had your lover, like another. The chaffing is gentle, and one senses a tenderness, beneath the deadpan humor, to the way that the voice considers our failed attempts to connect with our mates and would-be mates.

You are still the man in the backyard in Manitou Springs. You can never do anything right. And now she is really mad at you. People only get mad at you when they've got some silly reason to be mad. She is not even in the backyard anymore she is so mad. She will get over it. You know she will get over it. But you wish you didn't have to wait.

The sun is on the other side of the mountain, and you are growing cold. But not too cold. The dog looks up at you as you collect the plates and head inside, but he keeps chewing the bone. The fluorescent glow above the sink is not real. Pieces of fat and gristle are electrically disposed of and you don't want to think about where they go, what they become.

Do you look forward to settling down? Are you eager to stay put for a while? Are you ready to develop a sense of obligation? If you are, or if you do, then you will not make anyone believe that you are the man washing the dishes in the fluorescent light.

The series of questions parodies the flat, banal, uncaring language of the story problem. At this point, "you" and your problems are nothing more than ciphers, at least in "her" eyes. But the rueful comic voice gives expression to the kinds of serious, genuine questions that would go through a person's mind at a moment like this, making this cipher into an authentic character, as believable and graspable as more traditionally fleshed-out characters. The narration of this scene is much more effective than if Perkins had given names to the man and the woman, and staged them having a conventional fight, with him shouting "I just can't commit!" and her yelling back "If you plan to sleep here tonight, you'd better learn!"

STOCK PLOT, NEW VOICE

Perkins knows too well the pitfalls of this subject matter, which cries out for a fresh approach. He is keenly aware that no amount of scenic contrivance will disguise the familiarity of this topic. In itself, the couple's standoff seems as hackneyed as the scenario of some commedia dell'arte scenario out of the eighteenth century, where the peasant loves the princess but can't marry her because of his low birth. Then, he turns out to be a prince in disguise, who didn't know about his noble birth. He discovers his identity in the nick of time, just when he was sure that he and his sweetheart would never get together and overcome her father's objections.

Sound familiar? It should. Despite the fact that these stock plots were known in advance to playgoing audiences of that time, the ingenuity of the plays, and their language, made for

some of the most exciting theater of its era. The French playwrights Pierre de Marivaux and Molière, using the theatrical
equivalent of voice, created brilliant effects out of love situations that were dramatic clichés.

In composing my folk-based musical play, *The Devil in Disputanta,* I have had to contend with similar problems, though
on a slightly different plane. Appalachian and Southern folk
culture possesses some similar attitudes about this relation between originality and stock elements. Blues music, for instance,
doesn't always make clear distinctions about who particular
combinations of chords might "belong" to in terms of their
source, and the same is doubly true of the lyrics. How many
blues songs have you ever heard that begin with the phrase
"Woke up this morning . . ."? The same is true of hillbilly music, which not infrequently relies on the repetition of a single
chord progression for its mesmerizing effect.

That is not to say, however, that blues and hillbilly music
are not original. If you've ever attended a fiddlers' convention,
you know what the word "virtuoso" means in a folk context.
Red hot sounds come shooting out of virtually every fiddle.
Even though they all may be playing the same notes, the individual performance brings out a unique vision and version of a
song that is supposedly the same.

Appalachian folk tales and jokes operate with a similar set
of assumptions. The same particular anecdote may circulate
in the mouths of hundreds or thousands of people, but some
performances get a laugh or an appreciative nod, while others
leave the listeners stone-faced, unmoved. Everything depends
on the drawls, the pauses, the deadpan look on the face, with
just the hint of a twinkle behind the eyes. Sometimes the listeners have already heard the joke, perhaps more than once, but
that doesn't take away any of their relish, if they know it's going
to be retold to their satisfaction. They may start chuckling, an-
ticipating the punch line, as the teller rolls the words around
in her mouth, scratching her head, embellishing, pretending
that she can't remember exactly how it goes, or that she's making the whole thing up right on the spot. The audience knows
better, but they play along, knowing they'll get their payoff.

LISTEN TO THE SILVER-TONGUED DEVIL

In writing *The Devil in Disputanta*, I decided to use the Devil because he is perhaps the most familiar mythic figure in Appalachian folklore. It's also true that the Devil has made plenty of appearances throughout the history of world literature, in everything from Goethe's *Faust* to the book of Luke. My interest in using him sprang from my father's telling me the bit of lore that the Devil, in the farming town of Disputanta where my father was born, showed up in a place called the Hainted Holler at certain times to roll fireballs down the holler.

In the opening scene of the play, one of the characters runs into a pie auction to inform everyone that he has spotted the Devil doing just that, and that the tail of his horse has gotten singed as a result. The news causes a stir. Some believe the news and others disbelieve. The dramatic effect I'm able to wring from the Devil's presence in the play derives from letting him exist, for the most part, in rumors and gossip, without actually being seen. When he is seen, it's by only one person at a time, and for brief periods, so that his existence can't be proved or disproved. By the beginning of the second act, the audience is primed to see more of him, in the flesh.

Once he does make his sustained appearance, though, the problem for me becomes one of invention. The motif of the Devil tempting humans to sin is an ancient one, and every seemingly possible variation on it has been done. Again, voice provides a possible remedy. My solution has been, like the fiddler's, to focus on the instance of performance, on his gift for gab, but rooting his dialogue, like everyone else's, in the folk speech of the area where the play is set.

The suspense here, for the audience, lies not so much in not knowing what is going to happen, but rather in having a pretty good idea beforehand, and then watching the Devil and his prey each try to talk his way around the other one. The second character, an eighteen-year-old bootlegger and rounder named Taylor, doesn't realize who he's talking to, although the audience catches on quickly to the Devil's true identity. Taylor is waiting in the woods of the Hainted Holler for his fiancé

Verda, with whom he plans to elope. In mountain gospel music, such as the hymns of the Stanley Brothers, the Devil is sometimes referred to as "The Stranger," and that becomes his moniker in this scene of *Devil*. The possibility is left open that this being is no more or less than what he claims to be, a man from Arkansas who has trekked overland to get to Kentucky. As such, it's all the more important that the voice he's given to speak in sound eminently human, but with an ingredient added to it.

After overcoming their initial awkwardness about meeting unexpectedly in the woods, the two men cut themselves a plug of tobacco, strike up a conversation, and the stranger goes to work on Taylor.

Stranger (cutting a plug for himself): Waiting on somebody?

Taylor: My galfriend. She's got her ways.

Stranger: How so?

Taylor: We tied up our belongings and meant to ride clean out of the valley this morning, once and for all, once we made a little stop in Big Hill. And we hadn't rid but this far when she got a notion. Said she had to go say a proper goodbye to her daddy.

Stranger: They'll do that. I hope she didn't change her mind.

Taylor (defensive, almost haughty): I reckon not. Leastways, she better not have. That would be mean and low, leaving me here waiting.

Stranger: Yes, it would. But it happens. Sometimes you can shame the Devil without even meaning to. I'm a bit of an authority on that.

Taylor (sizing him up): Where did you say you was from?

Stranger: Didn't say. But I been living in Arkansas. Just came from there overland, fishing and hunting the whole way, sleeping in the woods. Slept here in this holler last night. Looks like I picked the likeliest time to come.

Taylor (smiling): You ought not of slept on this particular ground. Everybody in Disputanta says the Devil was walking up here last night, rolling fireballs down the holler.

Stranger: Is that so? Well, now, I settled down pretty late, I will say, but by the time I got situated there was nobody here but me, so far as I know.

Taylor: Folks around here can't rest easy unless they conjure up a boogerman first. I suppose it helps them enjoy church on Sunday. Foolishness, if you ask me.

Stranger: And what do you suppose the Devil looks like?

Taylor: Red, I reckon. If he existed. (Pondering) Then again, he could probably assume whatever shape he wanted. Being Lucifer and all. Law, what I wouldn't give to be able to do that. Would have saved me many a hasty mount onto my sorrel. Many a bruised tailbone. What brings you out to Disputanta?

Stranger: I used to live on Clear Creek, once upon a time. It's been twenty year ago now. I was married to Jenny Simpson.

Taylor (startled): Jenny Simpson! Don't you know she's a witch? (Composing himself) Leastways that's what everybody says. I don't believe a word of it. No offense, I hope.

Stranger: None taken. I hain't seen her in twenty years, so there's no telling what she's got into. Like as not she might be one.

Taylor: Everybody always talked about a feller she was wed to for a short time. A man she'd had a child by. Nobody knew where he came from, nor even his name. Said he only lived in Disputanta for a few weeks. I guess you're him.

Stranger: I guess I must be.

In this scene, the Devil fits in so well that there's no necessary reason for Taylor to doubt his identity. He cuts a plug of tobacco and uses laconic sayings of the kind a country man from Disputanta would: "They'll do that." His idiom stays so close to Taylor's, he is able to pass himself off as a former townsman.

If I had chosen to make The Stranger talk like a stranger, it would have violated the psychological and dramatic underpinnings of the scene. Taylor is naturally suspicious, and in trouble with the law at this point in the play. If he had detected a "foreign" accent on the Stranger's lips, the first thing he would have done is fight or flee. As it is, the Devil can begin to work his wiles on Taylor by adopting the local accent. This ploy in turn makes it possible for Taylor to conclude that the man is Jenny Simpson's former husband, and therefore a past member of the community. Appropriately, Taylor's last words in the scene, as the Stranger walks off, are "He was a silver-tongued devil. I never did even catch his name."

Like the Devil, you as a fiction writer must begin to learn when it is most expedient to sound like someone else, and when to sound like yourself. Temptation consists first of all in knowing what your victim wants, and setting up the promise that what he expects is what he'll get. Only then do you break the news that there has been a slight change of plan. There are times when by striving too hard to be unique, you end up betraying yourself. Your writing will always, at its best, be an intelligent combination of imitation and invention. It's much too easy to get caught up in the illusion that by finding the right topic, everything else will flow from there. Instead, try establishing a voice to envelop your character, and once that voice becomes sure, it will begin to dictate to you what you need to write about.

Exercises

1. Take a favorite story by a published author and write a scenario of its plot. Try to figure out, in a general way, what essential human story is being told. Now "rewrite" that story, employing a totally different narrating voice. Make your narrator first person, told by your story's protagonist.

2. Write a three-page scene, employing a narrator like the one in Hurston's *Their Eyes Were Watching God.* Try to make it speak "big," but without losing sight of the specifics of the characters whose lives it is describing. Control is your main object.

3. Create a monologue, in which you allow the speaker to have a "virtuoso" voice. Don't be concerned about the content of the monologue. Instead, try to capture the particular note that allows the storyteller to fascinate her listeners. Allow the voice much more freedom than you do in item 2.

CHAPTER 7

THE INFLUENCE
OF OTHER VOICES

LEARNING TO RECOGNIZE AND DESCRIBE the essence of other writers' styles is a crucial element in a writer's ability to create his
own style. This process, which may appear at first blush self-
evident, is not nearly so easy as it sounds. No matter how much
or how passionately we read the novels and collections of stories
of favorite authors, bringing the virtues of that writing over into
our own compositions requires a steadfast, cultivated awareness. The apprehension of style can be done intuitively, but
intuition is not always the most efficient route.

This lesson was brought home to me some years ago, when
I was enrolled in an MFA program. Every year, this program
brought in an illustrious visiting writer for a single semester
to teach a literature course. The visiting writer my first year
happened to be the distinguished Nebraska novelist Wright
Morris, author of *The Field of Vision*, *Plains Song* and many other
novels. At that point he was in his seventies, still ferociously
alert, and not in a mood to suffer the impertinences of a pack
of voracious whelps eager to suck at his literary teats. He'd been
to Paris in the twenties and thirties, stood outside the salon
where Gertrude Stein told Hemingway that remarks aren't literature, and climbed the stairs of the house where Henry James,
at his most famous, brilliant, continental and fat, had fallen
over backwards in his chair at a dinner party.

Morris had not only visited the shrines, but he himself was
a kind of austere shrine. He'd written not one, but two autobi-
ographies, and was at work on a third. We, his students, had

scarcely enough biography under our belts to fill up the "con-
tributor's paragraph" in the back of a literary journal. In short,
we were awed, though we sometimes made feeble quips about
his peculiarities, such as his tendency to dress in safari khakis,
to hide the fact of our epic inferiority. In spite of this awe, I
somehow worked up my courage to invite him to dinner with
my wife and myself at our crummy apartment in a high-rise
building in married student housing.

Mostly what I remember about the encounter is that I made
a curried lentil dish but forgot to set the yogurt out, and that
the knees of all three of us touched under the tiny formica
breakfast table. How thin were the legs of this septuagenarian
literary lion in safari pants, with his shock of white hair and
Boer mustache! And yet, he didn't give an inch under the table.
Over it, however, he softened for a few moments, after his fashion, as he told us how the tacky, secondhand furnishings, the
sad draperies, and the generally impecunious air made him
nostalgic for the days when he was cutting his teeth as a writer.

My happiness would have been complete if he had gotten
expansive, smoked a couple of cigars, drunk some brandy, and
fallen over backward in his chair. But gauging his sinewy frame,
I knew nothing of the sort was going to happen. Besides, there
was no brandy on hand. Callow youth that I was, I had served
Gallo jug wine to this cosmopolite who resided in Mill Valley,
in the heart of California wine country. I comforted myself by
rationalizing that if Hemingway had been sitting in that same
garage-sale chair, he would have relished the Gallo. It would
have reminded him of the countless liters of Spanish jug wine
that had been drunk by the protagonists in *The Sun Also Rises*
before they passed out.

Even after this evening of relative familiarity, Morris's presence was no less forbidding to me. A couple of times, I volun-
teered to take him grocery shopping, and as I wheeled the
grocery cart along the aisles of the Piggily Wiggily, he stopped
me, snatched a box of instant potatoes from the shelf, and as
if he were giving me instruction in the finer points of creating
minor characters with riveting tics, he informed me in a grave
voice, "John, these are superior spuds."

Given that he was a Nebraska man, and an obvious connoisseur of the products of America's breadbasket, I duly took note. I interpreted the remark as some sort of Zen koan, an enigma about writing that I would puzzle over, rather than question the master further. I knew better than to press the point after I'd once timidly asked him for a letter of recommendation for a student fellowship, only to have him answer, in the heartland twang that audibly thickened when he was annoyed, "Well, I could write a letter saying that you've walked through the door of my classroom several times without falling over." I could have been insulted, but I reminded myself that what was good enough for Henry James was good enough for me.

In the classroom, Wright Morris held forth for three straight hours each week without tiring. We asked few questions, and tried to make our note-taking as unobtrusive as possible. He'd supplied us with a reading list of those fiction writers he considered to be the crème de la crème of twentieth century writing. The list included Henry James (naturally), D.II. Lawrence, Sherwood Anderson, Gertrude Stein, Max Frisch, Thomas Mann, Virginia Woolf and various others. His lectures were good, and his expectations high. Once, when we ventured a few halfhearted complaints about the overabundance of hypotactic sentences in James's five hundred-page *The American Scene*, Morris looked us over, one by one, with the eye of a bird of prey about to devour its young, and said, in a voice of slow but withering impatience, "Ladies and gentlemen, are you telling me that you are simply not *up* to James?"

My first unforgettable lesson in the apprehension of voice and style was soon to follow. Morris had a theory about the "signature of style" that he expected us to master by the end of the semester. His idea was that the style of each of the most illustrious writers was unique and so self-evident, that only a fool, after some minimal practice, could fail to recognize it. He told us that our final exam would consist of a series of sentences and passages culled from the dozen or so novels we had read. Our task would be to identify the author and novel each passage had been taken from, and to situate the passage in the context in which it occurred.

The week of the final, we formed study groups, made up mock exams for each other, and in lengthy sessions of mutual coaching, we fared reasonably well. The day of the exam, however, was another story altogether, and the ending looked none too happy. When the passages were set before me, they all ran together like the ink on the copy of *The American Scene* that I'd dropped into the bathtub water by accident while reading because it was so heavy and I was so drowsy. I couldn't make head or tail of the quotations. When the exams were handed back, Wright Morris's evaluation of mine was as succinct and merciless as I'd come to expect. All of the passages I'd identified incorrectly (roughly three quarters of them) had been marked with an *X*. On the cover of the blue book, he'd drawn a series of concentric circles, with a human hand in the center, to indicate a drowning pool. Underneath, he made a single comment: "Oh, my. And such a nice lad."

Fortunately for me, my classmates had fared no better than I had. And fortunately for all of us, the director of the program persuaded Wright Morris to throw out the exam results. My formative humiliation in the classroom, however, eventually made me determined to offer in my own classes a more specific mechanism for apprehending and appropriating the voices of authors than the mere injunction to soak them up by reading a lot. Reading is crucial, but the next step is conscious imitation. Once you can consistently and methodically perceive and analyze the voices that animate the fiction of other writers, you will be close to being able to do so for yourself. Let me explain.

READING AS A WRITER

Most of us perform this process to some degree, but usually in a haphazard and unconscious way. The first change that must take place is to cultivate this process of "reading as a writer" more deliberately, with calculation. The Pakistani novelist Zulfikar Ghose, in *The Fiction of Reality*, speaks to this issue.

A sentence which one has written and which appears

to contain a neatly expressed thought often does so because its form resembles a sentence which impressed us
in a writer we happened to have been reading. One's belief
in one's own originality involves a lapse of memory: one
forgets, for the moment, that the new thought has only
sought to re-discover a language already lodged in the
mind by another writer and, during one's forgetfulness,
one's self-admiration is only an intenser admiration for
that writer.

Ghose's notion may seem radical, but it is really quite a com-
monsensical one. Our culture has become so wedded to a strict
and false idea of originality that an exaggerated premium gets
put on expressing, at all costs, one's "own" voice as early as
possible. The impulse to write, too often, gets divorced from
the need to keep reading. Typically, the nerves felt by beginning writers have a lot to do with their sense that they haven't
yet discovered a voice they can call their own. No one wants to
confront *Ulysses* or *Invisible Man* or *Huckleberry Finn* if he doesn't
have to.

   On the face of it, Ghose's way of putting things may sound
like a defeat for the fiction writer. But recognizing the limits
and constraints on one's own originality in fact frees you to
listen with greater attention to the fictional voices of the past
and present that ultimately will guide you to a voice you can
call your own. The ability to "re-discover a language already
lodged in the mind by another writer" can be one of the most
powerful of driving creative forces, once you learn how to manage it so that imitation isn't mechanical.

   Ghose suggests that when you approve of a sentence you've
turned, more likely than not what you're actually approving of
is the echo of a writer you've read somewhere along the way.
Amnesia induces a form of mild conceit, the belief that the
world begins with ourselves. Yet amnesia is also more than that,
for the "forgetfulness," ideally, gives way to recognizing the
style of the writer who "lodged" the thought, or the way of
expressing it, in your mind to begin with. Writing, from this
persepctive, consists of a series of homages. Rather than feeling

enslaved by this state of affairs, a fiction writer takes a more active approach, using imitation as a conscious and deliberate principle rather than a haphazard and unconscious tendency. Admiration for other writers goes beyond the mere appreciation of the aesthete or dilettante and becomes, instead, a principle of composition. The mastery of other voices paradoxically allows you to develop your own voice.

IMITATION AND EXPERIENCE

In the very first pages of the *Poetics*, Aristotle makes it absolutely clear that the *mimetic faculty*, or the ability to imitate, marks the beginning point of art. Our ability as humans to reconstruct what we perceive in the world gives us the power of creation. "The process of imitation is natural to mankind from childhood on. Man is differentiated from other animals because he is the most imitative of them, and he learns his first lessons through imitation, and we observe that all men find pleasure in imitations. . . . Men, having naturally been endowed with this gift from the beginning and then developing it gradually, finally created the art of poetry from their early improvisations."

But in order for us to make full use of Aristotle's ancient insight, we must first refine it. After all, we're trying to avoid too heavy a reliance on the content of our own experiences, so that the stylistic influence of other writers becomes available. Aristotle's concept of imitation sets out nature, or what we in more modern terms might call "experience," "life" or "reality," as the chief thing to be imitated. You've probably heard it said over and over that you should "draw from life," or "use your experience" when you write a story. Henry James gauges the success of a writer according to how well he has been able to "produce the illusion of life."

Let's think for a moment, though, what we mean when we talk about life. Much of modern philosophy has taken up the question of whether language describes and contains a reality that pre-exists "out there," or whether language to some extent actually creates that reality. Some thinkers have argued that the particular language we inherit and possess severely conditions and structures what we're able to experience. The Quechua Indians of South America, since pre-Columbian times, have cultivated dozens of varieties of potato, and have even more ways of preparing them. The lexicon surrounding "potato-ness" is therefore large, and any foreigner who lived among them would probably be astounded by the range and subtlety of how the topic of potatoes is discussed. Even though their dietary habits have changed somewhat over the centuries, and many other foods now compete with the potato, the language pre-existing and available for speaking of potatoes helps keep that vegetable in a central place within the culture.

When you hear or think the name of a color—blue, for instance—you bring to it a whole web of public and private associations, such that you can never have a direct perception of its "blueness," because that word-thing always stays enmeshed in a net of language. The novelist William Gass has in fact written an entire book centered around the word "blue," *On Being Blue.*

Blue pencils, blue noses, blue movies, laws, blue legs and stockings, the language of birds, bees, and flowers as sung by longshoremen, that lead-like look the skin has when affected by cold, contusion, sickness, fear; the rotten rum or gin they call blue ruin and the blue devils of its delirium; Russian cats and oysters, a withheld or imprisoned breath, the blue they say that diamonds have, deep holes in the ocean and the blazers which English athletes earn that gentlemen may wear; afflictions of the spirit—dumps, mopes, Mondays—all that's dismal—low-down gloomy music, Nova Scotians, cyanosis, hair rinse, bluing, bleach; the rare blue dahlia like that blue moon shrewd things happen only once in, or the call for trumps in whist (but who remembers whist or what the death of unplayed games is like?), and correspondingly the flag, Blue Peter, which is our signal for getting underway; a swift pitch, Confederate money, the shaded slopes of clouds and mountains, and so the constantly increasing absentness of Heaven (*ins Blaue hinein,* the Germans say), consequently the color of everything that's empty: blue bottles, bank accounts, and compliments, for instance, or, when the sky's turned turtle, the blue-green bleat of ocean (both the same), and, when in Hell, its neatly landscaped rows of concrete huts and gas-blue flames; social registers, examination booklets, blue bloods, balls, and bonnets, beards, coats, collars, chips, and cheese . . . the pedantic and censorious . . . watered twilight, sour sea: through a scrambling of accidents, blue has become their color, just as it's stood for fidelity.

As Gass ticks off his catalog of blue, what intrigues us is not only the brilliance of his associations and their seeming originality, but how many of those associations we share with him, indeed what common territory our language turns out to be. He may express his thoughts in a way not so easy to duplicate, but he has decidedly tapped into the public reservoir of language, rather than some privately-owned and unadulterated well. In a more telescoped way, Gass does what we should all do in our writing—acknowledge our debt to the history of the language we pretend to "own," even as we try to renew it and to create patterns unlike any ever seen before. Gass is one of the more dazzling stylists of our time, but he achieves this effect by a calculated effort to strike plenty of familiar chords.

BEYOND PARODY

This attentiveness to the past of our language becomes still more focused when we begin the work of bringing the lessons of another writer over into our own fiction. Lee Smith has acknowledged her debt to Faulkner in her novel *Oral History*, yet with a difference. In using some of the lessons of his style, she goes beyond a derivative impulse. By being selective, she creates an effect that becomes in the end her own, although its point of departure can easily be traced to the novel *Absalom, Absalom!* That Faulkner novel treats familiarity and strangeness as it exists between men and women, blacks and whites. Rapprochements are difficult for Faulkner's characters to achieive, and the psychic pressure of remaining separate is rendered in the fluid but tense quality of his sentences.

Because Faulkner's sentences are so highly formed, so wrought, it is likely for them to become overwrought when they hit slightly off the mark. The formality of his prose, set against the sometimes earthy feel of his characters, with their over-heated sense of guilt, sexuality, decayed family honor, Southern identity, is just what makes Faulkner's prose easy pickings for parody. He is probably one of the most parodied writers, such as in the Univeristy of Mississippi's annual Faulkner contest, which gives a prize for the most skillful "good-bad" imitation of Faulkner.

Naturally, it is not really that difficult to parody Faulkner for a few sentences, and that sort of dubious homage, while good sport, doesn't take one very far along the road to under-standing what lies at the heart of Faulkner's writing. Lee Smith, while also indulging in a sophisticated kind of parody, carries out a more searching and thorough appropriation of Faulk-ner's style, which she sustains for seventy-five pages, in the long-est section of *Oral History.* To understand this particular in-stance of influence, let us first recall a typical passage of Faulkner's *Absalom, Absalom!* Its protagonist, Rosa Coldfield, at one point remembers a childhood encounter she had with Cly-tie in the house while searching for Judith. This brief meeting, as so often in Faulkner, gets played for all it is worth, and fairly drips with history and philosophy.

> I know only that my entire being seemed to run at blind full tilt into something monstrous and immobile, with a shocking impact too soon and too quick to be mere amazement and outrage at that black arresting and untim-orous hand on my white woman's flesh. Because there is something in the touch of flesh with flesh which abrogates, cuts sharp and straight across the devious intricate chan-nels of decorous ordering, which enemies as well as lovers know because it makes them both:—touch and touch of that which is the citadel of the central I-Am's private own: not spirit, soul; the liquorish and ungirdled mind is any-one's to take in any darkened hallway of this earthly

tenement. But let flesh touch with flesh and watch the fall of all the eggshell shibboleth of caste and color too.

Faulkner takes the hard road to telling us that Rosa's personal space has been violated and that there's not much she can do about it. His latinate phrases ("arresting and untimorous," "devious intricate channels of decorous ordering"); his use of euphemism and indirection ("something monstrous and immobile"); his flamboyant modifiers ("liquorish and ungirdled mind"); his philosophical outbursts ("the central I-Am's private own"); and his tendency to use complicated or compound sentences with plenty of subordinate clauses—all these hallmarks of style serve to ratchet up the emotional tension of the scene. Strictly speaking, not much happens, but a sense of foreboding, of impending disaster, of violated taboos about to be revealed, hangs in the air. Chronic nervous tension is the normal state of mind of Faulkner's characters. They're either going to tell you about the South, or bust trying to hold it in.

Faulkner in the Appalachians

None of this is lost on Lee Smith. In an interview, she once said "I love to write like Faulkner, but I can't do it straight." And yet, in *Oral History* she accomplishes much more than a knockoff of *Absalom, Absalom!* in her depiction of the nerve-wracked interloper Richard Burlage. Burlage is from Tidewater, Virginia, of aristocratic and educated background, a sort of Quentin Compson of the upper South, and strictly out of his depth in Hoot Owl Holler, the Appalachian backwater where the novel is set. In effect, Smith has taken a character straight out of Faulkner, and put him in an incongruous setting. In Faulkner, the white trash and the blacks are held at a distance, either consigned to the role of minor characters and manservants to the lapsed aristocracy, or, in the case of the Snopeses, tacitly or overtly disapproved of within the narrative structure as a whole.

But in Smith's novel, things shake down differently. The hillbillies not only have the upper hand vis à vis Richard, but they also have a more fundamental and enduring understanding of the vital forces that set them in motion. They know who they are. Richard Burlage, on the other hand, is paralyzed by self-consciousness. His thoughts and impressions appear in journal entries. The more he writes, and the greater his urgency to "get it all down," the more he dooms himself to failure and misunderstanding because of his desire to analyze everything rather than experience it. He has gone to be a schoolteacher in a mountain schoolhouse, but his tendency to judge others in haste, and his conviction that these poor yokels need to be helped by his superior knowhow, so they can be brought up to his level, ensure that he will remain an outsider. The one person he most desperately needs to save, of course, is himself.

Smith spins out his journal entries with relish, obviously enjoying the license to overwrite which she has granted herself through this character voice, yet never losing sight of her purpose for the novel as a whole.

> Enough, enough. I have written away the end of the afternoon. From my window I look down upon the sleepy town square surrounded as it is by these harsh mountains. I see the shopkeepers locking up now and heading home, an occasional bright leaf spiraling downward to land unnoticed upon a sober dark hat, a somber coat. Why do I want to weep? Earlier today Mrs. Poole said I look "plumb tuckered out," and yet my nerves feel so jangled that I am certain I shall never sleep again. I have the sense of standing upon some precipitous verge which will alter the course of my life. I believe in God, yes—Victor notwithstanding. I believe in the Father, Son, and Holy Ghost. I believe that nothing happens at random, that we all of us fill a role in His master plan. . . . Are these, indeed, portents? What do they signify?

Like Quentin Compson in *Absalom, Absalom!*, Burlage turns each observation over relentlessly in his mind in the hope that it will yield up its hidden meaning. Each insignificant detail seems to send him into a fit of self-doubt, like an inexperienced hound that thinks he's treed a fox, but keeps looking back to his master for confirmation. Smith doesn't, however, play

Burlage strictly for laughs. It's true that he is viewed critically, in the end, for his lack of perspective, and most of all because of his faint-heartedness in failing to return the love and devotion of Dory, the mountain girl with whom he has a fling.

At the same time, Smith endows Burlage with a keen capacity for observing details, even when he misses the overall picture, such as when he visits a Primitive Baptist church and is impressed (albeit a little condescendingly) by the simple faith of the worshippers, and their willingness to offer him hospitality. In the interest of her story and its dramatic involvement, Lee Smith also allows Richard to be drawn, however briefly, into the immediacy of a love experience, where his irony and supposed intellectual superiority are perforce thrown aside. Because of these added touches, we begin to see Richard as human and dimensional, on a par with the others, rather than simply seeing him as a pale Faulknerian intruder with no organic relation to the story being told.

Parody gives way to character. In one of the novel's more touching scenes, Richard finds himself alone at the schoolhouse, where he sleeps. A flood is impending, and Dory arrives to alert him to clear out before the creek overflows. When she enters the cabin, the barely submerged sexual attraction between the two starts to show itself, and they profess their love for each other in plainspoken language.

> We stood before the stove, we two, in this empty schoolhouse, while rain fell steadily on the roof and the creek roared past outside. The schoolhouse was dim, warm. Dory's wet wool clothing gave off a peculiar kind of smell—pleasant, really—which will stay in my mind forever. For once I had nothing to say. I held her close, I stroked her hair. And then I felt my manhood rising unawares, and died of shame and a kind of glory as I realized she must feel it too, pressing against her body.
>
> "Honey," she said. Who would have thought that anyone would ever address me so? She kissed me, opening her mouth.
>
> "Dory." It was all I could say. Kissing we made our way to my bed in the corner where we sat, or fell, in a

kind of heat, and she leaned back and pulled me to her. I fumbled at her waist and finally succeeded in pulling up her blouse—to my surprise, she wears no brassiere! Or maybe none of these mountain girls do. Her breasts are the most perfect breasts which exist in all the world!

At this point, Lee Smith is clearly not in the thrall of Faulkner. She uses his style with deliberation, and curtails it when it gets in the way of her own purposes. In this scene, Burlage appears very much a Lee Smith creation. Her characters tend to be impulsive, passionate, and for all their love of words, their talk is for the most part about immediate concerns, immersed in the flow of moment-to-moment living. There is something sweet and schoolboyish, almost charming, about Burlage's excitement coupled with his naïveté. His "sophistication" has dropped away to reveal not only an innocence in sexual matters, but also, and more importantly, the ability to feel and be moved by love.

Still, Smith keeps him tethered to the conception of character that she has created for him. When he generalizes, speculating that "maybe none of these mountain girls do" wear brassieres, there is a hint of the callow, standoffish Richard Burlage who will ultimately reject Dory's passionate simplicity, and opt instead for the studied coquettishness of his fiancée back in Richmond. By allowing Richard Burlage at least a passing acquaintance with the full range of human emotions and motivations, and by tempering his voice—most other sections of *Oral History* are narrated by the inhabitants of Hoot Owl Holler—with the voices of Appalachians, Lee Smith allows for the influence of Faulkner without having it become an oppressive weight on her own style.

THE SORCERER'S APPRENTICE

The question of influence is a complicated one. There are, at any given time, many authors whose presence in some way bleeds into your own style. At certain junctures, one author will consume you more than others, and you'll feel that you need to process his work as fully as you can before you move on to someone else. When someone asks me who has influenced a particular work of mine, I'm often at a loss to say. At different times of my life, I have contracted a literary crush that during that phase seemed exclusive, for the fiction of writers as diverse as D.H. Lawrence, John Barth, Henry James, Teresa Porzecanski, Flannery O'Connor, Katherine Anne Porter, Walker Percy. Each time, I really did mean to be faithful, but in the end I was promiscuous.

Some of them, such as D.H. Lawrence, I can hardly abide to read anymore, while others, such as Katherine Anne Porter, I can always go back to with fresh pleasure. There was a period when I could scarcely write a sentence without it sounding like something Walker Percy had discarded at the end of the day. Now, I only seek insight consistently in one of his novels. And who is this Teresa Porzecanski, who suddenly popped up in the midst of a discussion on minor characters? Is she herself a minor character, or a major one? My answer is that I still correspond with her where she lives in Uruguay, and she sends me a copy of each new work as it appears in print, because my appetite for her work is inexhaustible (so far).

When I first picked up a short story by Flannery O'Connor, I couldn't stop reading until I had consumed everything by her I could get my hands on, including her correspondence and her occasional essays. At present, I find her worldview too harsh and unrelenting, her style too angular to suit me. All the same, she did her number on me at the time when I was receptive to it. One doesn't think of being smitten by Flannery O'Connor. But I was—perhaps more in the way that one warrior smites another over the head with a scepter than the way the beloved endears her lover. All I know is that despite myself, my ears still sometimes ring with the cadences of her prose.

The lesson in all this is that influence, like a dropped nickel, lies wherever you find it and wherever you take the trouble to bend over long enough to pick it up. Once you become attuned to the inner rhythms of a writer, you'll be surprised at how quickly you can learn at least some of the lessons that author has to offer. And, in a few cases, if you're diligent and lucky, you'll master a large number of them. The fiction of your artistic mentors doesn't change over time, but your relationship to it as apprentice will. The important thing is to always be in the midst of cultivating at least one fictional relationship in an intensive way. Like the friendships and loves in your life, your fictional apprenticeships will vary in intensity and duration.

And not all writers are alike in this way. For some, two or three writers will hold sway over them for years, perhaps even most of their life. For others, to dwell with a single writer for an entire year may seem a long time. There is no single right approach to this question, except always to keep some guiding fiction close at hand, and to resist the temptation to read writers chiefly in anthology format. Anthologies have their place, but they never provide you with more than a passing glance at an author's work. It is necessary to have a deep and thorough acquaintance with the corpus of fiction of at least a couple of writers in order for "influence" to become a real possibility.

REMAKING YOURSELF

The other thing to remember is not to set limits on who you think you can or ought to be influenced by. Whatever your sex, ethnicity, social class or region, you can learn from a broad array of fictional guides. Don't stint your ambition by deciding in advance that only certain kinds of writing can be good for you. The timid student is the one who declares beforehand the limits on what she is willing to learn.

Because much of my own scholarship, and some of my teaching, lies within what has come to be known as "multicultural studies," I am very much alive to the need of a writer to tap as directly as possible into the stream of traditions that issues from his own race, region, etc. That is a necessary and important part of the formative experience of coming to artistic maturity. For years, my own need to come closer to my Appalachian heritage has grown, and those preoccupations in crucial ways now reside at the center of my creative endeavor. At the same time, I remain open and actively searching in my continuing exploration of South American and European writing, as well as more ancient traditions.

For my money, one of the most intelligent commentators on this question in recent times is the novelist Charles Johnson, author of the outstanding short story collection *The Sorcerer's Apprentice,* who also won the National Book Award for his novel *Middle Passage.* Johnson is a black fiction writer who has learned as much from Chaucer and Dostoievski as he has from Ralph Ellison and Ntozake Shange. For him, it is not a question of either/or. His work says, "I choose all."

Johnson exhorts writers to make greater use of indirect experience, to intuit other lives. That is simply his way of putting greater emphasis on what fiction writers always have to do. We have to write about men and women, young and old, people from different social classes. Johnson asks us, in addition, to be more alive to other cultural traditions. He is specifically responding to the tendency of black writers during the sixties and seventies to deal almost exclusively with black characters.

Yet it's a two-way street. There was a huge controversy when William Styron's novel *The Confessions of Nat Turner* was awarded the Pulitzer Prize. But Johnson no doubt applauded the attempt of a white writer to make a historical black character who led a slave revolt the protagonist of his novel, because in theory at least, the task forces Styron to, as Johnson says, "divest himself of his own historically acquired peculiarities, and reconstruct his world."

Johnson's view would be that regardless of our particular race, sex, etc.; as writers, the historical figure Nat Turner is equally distant from all of us. As such, we have to *remake* him, and that process allows us to both criticize an alien persepctive, and, at the same time, remake our own. In his essay "Being and Fiction," Johnson specifically says:

> Doubters may object that it is racially impossible to strip themselves of their own historically acquired traits. Many black writers claim they cannot imagine what it is like to be white, that all they know is the "black" experi-

ence. For my money, this objection is sheer laziness. I will also say that such objections are based on a very circumscribed notion of race. . . . Our lives as blacks and whites are a tissue of cross-cultural influences.

His challenge is issued as much to white, Native American, Chicano, and other writers as to blacks. One interesting example of what he's talking about could be the work of the writer Leslie Marmon Silko. She herself is of mixed ancestry: Laguna Pueblo, Mexican and white, and so this sort of cross-fertilization of perspectives comes naturally to her. In her beautiful novel *Ceremony*, her protagonist, a young, mixed-blood male Laguna named Tayo, was once a Japanese prisoner of war, and then returned to his reservation. He tries to come to terms with his conflicted identity. Silko mixes realistic description and dialogue about modern life with visionary dream states, ceremonial chants and Indian folk tales. Silko opens the novel by having the various competing voices converge in Tayo's head as he lies in bed.

Tayo didn't sleep well that night. He tossed in the old iron bed, and the coiled springs kept squeaking even after he lay still again, calling up humid dreams of black night and loud voices rolling him over and over again like debris caught in a flood. Tonight the singing had come first, squeaking out of the iron bed, a man singing in Spanish, the melody of a familiar love song, two words again and again, "*Y volveré.*" Sometimes the Japanese voices came first, angry and loud, pushing the song far away, and then he could hear the shift in his dreaming, like a slight afternoon wind changing its direction, coming less and less from the south, moving into the west, and the voices would become Laguna voices, and he could hear Uncle Josiah calling to him, Josiah bringing him the fever medicine when he had been sick a long time ago. But before Josiah could come, the fever voices would drift and whirl and emerge again—Japanese soldiers shouting orders to him, suffocating damp voices that drift out in the jungle stream, and he heard the women's voices then; they faded in and

out until he was frantic because he thought the Laguna
words were his mother's, but when he was about to make
out the meaning of the words, the voice suddenly broke
into a language he could not understand; and it was then
that all the voices were drowned by the music—loud, loud
music from a big juke box, its flashing red and blue lights
pulling the darkness closer.

THE WAY FROM GAY TO HEMINGWAY

This is only one of many techniques for going deeply into a
relative perspective. Once I filled in for a creative writing colleague on a day she was teaching Ernest Hemingway's story
"The Snows of Kilamanjaro." A number of the students in the
class, obviously feeling they had nothing to lose by complaining
to the "temp," let me know in no uncertain terms that they
didn't care for Hemingway, and found him misogynistic, insen-
sitive to other cultures, and too filled with cheap machismo to
be taken seriously—the usual complaints levelled against Hemingway, and to some extent just. A young black lesbian woman
felt especially out of sympathy with the story, feeling that it
could in no way speak to her concerns.

I told them that I frankly wasn't much of a Hemingway
aficionado myself, in part because his vision of things was too
discrepant with my own, but that they were squandering an
opportunity if they didn't recognize his technical finesse, and
didn't try to profit from it, since they were reading him already.
I thought of a novelist friend of mine, Arturo Islas, who died
of AIDS in the early 1990s, just as he was beginning to achieve
fame as a novelist. In many respects, Islas couldn't have been
more different from Hemingway: gentle, soft-spoken, Chicano,
gay, fiercely protective of his private life. And yet, Hemingway
and F. Scott Fitzgerald were his literary masters, and he was
fond of reminding people of that fact. The books of these two
celebrated authors were always prominently featured in his
courses on modern literature at Stanford.

Islas was intensely committed to cultivating and helping

promote Chicano writing as a distinct presence within American writing. But like Charles Johnson, he did not find the goal of "ethnic" or "gay" writing incompatible with availing oneself of the full range of what U.S. (and world) culture had to offer. In his view, to see gays or Chicanos as wholly separate from other people in their range of life concerns was to stereotype them in the worst way.

One of the features that in fact unites Hemingway and Islas is their view of human sexuality and human relations as often mercenary. The temptation to cheapen one's emotions to satisfy a craving for love is better described as a human foible than as an exclusively gay one. And coming from Chicano culture, Islas understood as well as anyone, including Hemingway, the pulse of machismo that often regulates male attitudes toward sexuality.

At their best, these two authors are exploratory and not cynical, because even when they see humans as mercenaries, they are mercenaries by default. Those characters search for tenderness, and they end up settling for inferior, inadequate replacements for the affection they fail to find, in order to keep fear and loneliness from overtaking their lives. These insights get conveyed in the two authors' prose fiction in a characteristic fashion. Hemingway is usually lapidary, almost brusque, and he doesn't shy away from using a summary style to express ongoing tics of behavior that the protagonist is trying hard to come to terms with.

In "The Snows of Kilamanjaro," Harry has contracted a fatal case of gangrene through a trivial oversight, by not attending to a scratch on his leg that becomes infected. This haphazardness seems appropriate to the way he conducts his affairs in general. To be a man is to not give a damn about how things turn out—or at least to pretend that's the way you feel. Things begin simply enough, and turn destructive by degrees. The same cavalier attitude is true of his relationship with the unnamed woman who is his lover and companion now, and who has accompanied him on a safari to Africa.

It had begun very simply. She liked what he wrote and

she had always envied the life he led. She thought he did exactly what he wanted to. The steps by which she had acquired him and the way in which she had fallen in love with him were all part of a regular progression in which she had built herself a new life and he had traded away what remained of his old life.

He had traded it for security, for comfort too, there was no denying that, and for what else? He did not know. She would have bought him anything he wanted. He knew that. She was a damned nice woman too. He would as soon be in bed with her as any one; rather with her, because she was richer, because she was very pleasant, and because she never made scenes.

The portrait of Harry is anything but flattering. Close to death, he systematically, if subjectively, tries to admit to himself the pettiness, the series of compromises, the grabbing after some semblance of stability that has little by little taken over his existence. One might say that this is the only true moment of bravery in a life devoted to big game hunting, hard drinking, womanizing and generally toughing it out. At times he blames the woman for his downfall, at times himself. Harsh criticisms have been levelled against Hemingway's stories by some people, but writers are surely not bound to give an idealized view of characters' motivations and psyches. Indeed, one of the things I admire about Arturo Islas's novel *The Rain God* is the tone of sympathy pervading the prose, yet Islas is not the least averse to displaying his characters' secret perversions, adulteries and self-deceptions.

One of the principals in *The Rain God* is Felix, a middle-aged, married but bisexual Chicano who eventually meets a violent death at the hands of a young soldier he picks up. Felix, who can be seen as in some respects an alter ego for the author, is portrayed with tenderness on Islas's part. But Islas does not hesitate to reveal a view of sexuality as casually corrupt, in much the same vein as Hemingway. The fact that one author deals with the underside of heterosexual relations and the other with the underside of homosexual ones simply means a change of emphasis, not a distinction of kind. And Islas is able to make his portrait of Felix as a gay man convincing precisely by considering him as a whole human being, with a professional and family identity as well as a sexual one. He is Mama Chona's son, he is gay, and he is a foreman.

> The Mexicans he hired reminded Felix of himself at that age, men willing to work for any wage as long as it fed their families while strange officials supervised the preparation of their papers. As middleman between them and the promises of North America, he knew he was in the loathsome position of being what the Mexicans called a *coyote*; for that reason he worked hard to gain their affection.
>
> A person of simple and generous attachments, Felix loved these men, especially when they were physically strong and naive. Even after losing most of his own hair and the muscles he had developed during his early years on the job, he had not lost his admiration for masculine beauty. As he grew older that admiration, instead of diminishing as he had expected, had become an obsession for which he sought remedy in simple and careless ways.
>
> Before they were permitted to become full-time employees, the men were required to have physical examinations. . . . The physical consisted of tests for hernias and prostate trouble and did not go beyond that unless the young worker, awareness glinting at him with his trousers down, expressed an interest in more. The opportunists figured that additional examinations might be to their advantage, although Felix did not take such allowances into account later. In those brief morning and afternoon encounters, gazing upon such beauty with the wonder and terror of a bride, his only desire was to touch it and hold it in his hands tenderly.

Islas has brought over from Hemingway the insight that people are often willing to bargain away their sexuality in subtle ways for reasons of varying complexity. They may be cheap, but they are not whores. Islas's simile, "with the wonder and terror of a bride," because it is unexpected, implicating both parties in the exchange, seems psychologically accurate.

Felix's role as foreman or *coyote* plays a large part in his conception of himself and his relation to the workers. Strangely, the ruse of giving physical exams is driven as much by his desire to relate to his workers and ingratiate himself to them (by later doing favors for them and their families) as it is by his lust. And within the novel as a whole, Felix's story becomes only a piece of the family mosaic. The fact that he is Mama Chona's son counts for more, as far as the family is concerned, than the fact that he is bisexual. He will be quarreled with and mourned, in the end, in much the same way as the swaggering *machos* he calls his uncles and cousins.

The influence of other writers is a necessary and desireable part of the development of your own voice. Even experienced writers like Lee Smith and Arturo Islas take pains to draw on the experiences of their artistic predecessors and contemporaries. As you continuously keep your eyes trained on the lessons of one author or another, you will at some point glance down at the page containing your own scrawl and delight yourself when you find that you have developed a style you can call your own. Wright Morris never told me so directly, but I figured out along the way that it's possible to be a nice lad and a good writer too.

Exercises

1. Make a list of some of your pet words, ones that most fascinate you. Write a paragraph for each in which you explore both the private and public associations each word has for you within your own vocabulary.

2. Choose a writer whose work especially challenges you. Engage in the kind of sophisticated parody of that writer that Smith or Islas employs. You don't have to be completely respectful and reverential, but the point isn't to achieve just a comic knockoff of that writer either. How might you appropriate cadences, registers of language, syntax, tones, offered by that writer for your own devious purposes?

3. In a scene or series of scenes, strive to "divest yourself"

and "reconstruct yourself" in the way Johnson suggests. Choose a character who you might not normally think to create, one who is different enough from yourself to stretch all of your preconceptions.

CHAPTER 8

MANY VOICES, ONE VOICE

NOW THAT YOU HAVE BEGUN TO APPRECIATE the possibilities of the narrative, dramatic and authorial voices separately, it is time to think about working with them in concert. Yet care must be taken with the meanings we allow ourselves to attach to the word "concert." Too often, artists make equivocal analogies between creative writing and music. In poetry, especially, the poet is cast as a cantor, a vatic presence apt to burst unprovoked into ethereal song at any moment. This image of the writer as a bard comes as much as anything from the notion of writing as a vocation something like a religious calling. This concept has bled over into fiction writing as well, so that the the fiction writer figures, mistakenly, as an unaccompanied soloist whose cri de coeur initiates us, her listeners, into an audible understanding of the human condition.

Yet, as we have begun to see, the voices available to a novelist, even a short story writer, are multiple, sometimes myriad. The illusion of "a" voice is not only difficult to sustain—at times, one can scarcely isolate the single voice controlling all the rest who sound off within the space of a composition. In part, this illusory search is fed by our culture's exaggerated preoccupation with "uniqueness"—the belief that one's voice print has to be sole, separate, and, like an obscene phone call, instantly and easily traced. The seamlessness that might seem appetizing to a certain kind of lyric poet, to a fiction writer can be nothing less than monotonous. One need only remember the etymological root of "monotone" to understand this insight. The Greek *monos tonos*, which already begins to sound repetitive to the ear the first time we hear it uttered, means one tone, one sound, a chant in a single tone—monos tonos, monos tonos, monos tonos.

You might also keep in mind that it was religious denominations such as the Shakers who believed that the unaccompanied human voice came the closest one could come to expressing the essence of God. But though the Shakers have bequeathed to us some of the most beautiful—and briefest—psalms ever chanted at sunrise on rolling pasture land, we would be hard pressed to name a single Shaker novelist. When it comes to voice, simplicity serves less as a part of the fiction writer's vocabulary than does multiplicity.

The ban on musical instruments practiced by the Shakers would not stand us fiction writers in very good stead at the moment we are called to rehearse the narrative, dramatic and authorial voices in concert. If the musical analogy holds at all, one would need to describe the act as more symphonic than bardic. And that symphony would more likely than not take the form of a polyphonic, cantankerous grouping, seventy-six trombones given to misrule, along with various prima donnas, not just one, preening, upstaging, clamoring for the conductor's attention, throwing egomaniacal tantrums, and generally making themselves disagreeable.

Yet no matter how much the prosaic prima donnas might annoy, the task of the novelist or short story writer is to *rehearse* those voices, in both senses of the word. First, to perfect them so that over time they begin to work in harmony with one another, producing a pleasing unity of effect. Second, to try the voices out, in the sense that one says "I'm going to rehearse this story to you," tell it or recite it to you. That is, the conductor must give the varied voices sufficient free rein, while not letting them run roughshod over him, but also without sacrificing or dismissing any of them either. It's a thankless job, but one that has to be performed nonetheless. If you do it right, people will take your skill for granted, and if you mess it up, everyone will be ready to criticize you for your slipshod managerial style.

The phrase "in concert," then, refers less to fantasies of

celestial musical harmony, less to the humility of flawless Gregorian chants and sunny Shaker hymns, and more to the *concerted* effort the novelist has to make to give all the voices their simultaneous due, all the while somehow keeping them in check. That isn't to say that fiction writers seek total cacophony. Like the lyric poets, we too have our symmetries, our euphonies and our harmonies. If our words crowd the pages, murmuring scales under their breath, they do so in an orderly fashion. But the pleasure of the novelist is often that of the errant blast, the erratic note that strays through the open window from the street, shattering our comfortable domestic bliss, our fireside reveries.

TOOTING THE KLAXON

One summer, I decided to spend a weekend at Pleasant Hill, the Shaker colony located out a winding rural route in central Kentucky, past horse farms, yearlings and fieldstone walls that predate the Civil War. Though Pleasant Hill exists only twenty-five minutes away from my birthplace, I had managed never to visit it during my growing up years, in the way that one forsakes the museum around the corner to visit instead, at great expense and with complicated travel arrangements, the Acropolis or Machu Picchu. The Shaker colony, long since abandoned by its first utopian inhabitants, who believed in the virtues of celibacy and song, has been lovingly restored over the past couple of decades to something approaching its original splendor, with all due historical care.

What most impresses one about the site, on arrival, is that it has managed to remain, in its new incarnation, almost entirely free of kitsch. The curators have resisted the temptation to load down the grounds with tacky billboards, circa circus whirligigs and cutesy-pie Americana. Those who work there dress in the chaste original garb, but they don't push their luck by pasting on fake accents. After all, we know they're married with a passel of kids. For the most part, those who work at Pleasant Hill are local craftspeople who understand very well how to work a lathe or run the shuttle of a loom. If they're not farmers, they're the sons and daughters of farmers, with a certain pioneer tang still on their breaths.

As they say in the brochures, the rooms of the dining hall, filled with original Shaker sideboards and tables or matchless reproductions, offer a blend of Shaker recipes and contemporary regional specialties, big helpings family style and at a reasonable price. The dormitories that used to belong, respectively, to the men and the women, who slept apart and kept a celibate life, have been converted into low-key lodgings for overnight guests, and the colony is set on a couple of hundred acres of the original, softly undulating farmland next to the Kentucky River. In short, they've concocted an excellent knock-off of what the more pleasant aspects of Pleasant Hill must have felt like.

I must confess to a weakness for this sort of thing—hiatus with agreeable amenities. Like many another who has suffered disenchantments along the way, I yearn for the sacred, and need to stage a retreat from time to time. And in addition to the more strictly religious connotations of the place, the natural landscape of my birth and youth has always given me an almost primeval thrill. No terrain excites my blood more than the aerial approach to the Bluegrass Airport, passing over the white fences and horse pastures surrounding Lexington. And as a boy, I rode my bicycle down that airport road many a time to watch the planes come in, back when the hangar was still a Quonset hut set out among the cows. Before I knew that the Clinch Mountain Boys' rendition of the hymn "I'll Pass Over Thee" had to do with Jehovah's sacrificial instructions to Moses, I always thought that hymn was about a plane ride over the pastures of central Kentucky. Wasn't that why they called the music "bluegrass"?

So, rising in my first early morning at Pleasant Hill to walk down to the river, I inhaled the scent of fog lying in the bottomland, refracting the dawn sunlight, the tilled fields already high with tasseled corn and tobacco, and the outbuildings of the Shaker Village arrayed at a respectful, aesthetic distance from one another. If you approach the experience right, the place truly offers itself to contemplation. At eleven, church bells ring merrily throughout the grounds, calling those who wish, over-night lodgers and day guests alike, to a scaled-down reenact-ment of a Shaker meeting. When I entered the meeting house, two sets of unvarnished, backless pews faced one another, in former times used to segregate male and female worshippers.

The tourist crowd filling the pews had not segregated ac-cording to sex, but most of them, while unchastely intermin-gled, had demurely set their cameras in their laps, in a kind of unconscious reverence for their surroundings. The midmorn-ing light played against the sleek wood interior with its vaulted ceiling, yet still on a human scale, and I knew that I had entered a holy place. The "service" consisted of a single, spirited man who gave a monologue about the sanctuary's history, interspers-ing his words with lusty a capella renditions of hymns, along with the dance steps that served as their only accompaniment. No musical instruments adulterated his clear cantor's baritone.

For the Shakers, who eschewed carnal relations, this sanctu-ary meeting provided the only time and space for their ecstatic excesses, through dance and song, the rhythmic, symmetrical movements of body and soul.

> Welcome here, welcome here
> All be alive and be of good cheer.
>
> Come life, Shaker life, come life eternal
> Shake, shake out of me all that is carnal.

As I listened to the man's chant, my vision strayed to the occu-pants of the front row opposite, until my gaze alighted on the woman seated directly across from me. On her squat, middle-aged frame, she wore a bright, canary yellow T-shirt with the word HOOTERS emblazoned across the front. Ah, Hooters, that quintessentially American franchise of leering T&A! Redo-lent with extraordinary bad taste as this instant was, it made for a classic novelistic moment. The moment only could have been crowned by having a tuba player leap alongside the cantor, giving out a lusty blast to punctuate the phrase "all that is carnal." And made even better, in addition, if a car had roared down the rural route, in concert with that instant, playing "La Cucaracha" on its klaxon horn. Only, then, truly, would we have departed from the realm of the psalmodic and fully entered into the multiple voices of the novelistic. For the poet, there remains the unaccompanied human voice, instrument of God. For the novelist, the tooting of hooters. We are defined, for better or for worse, by the one voice that is many and the many voices that are one.

THE SIMPLE SENTENCE

As a teacher, my ideal is to make sophisticated ideas easier to grasp, while sacrificing as few of their nuances as I can. The imperative is to make the complex simple. As a fiction writer, however, that goal can come about, not by eliminating any of the three voices I've been describing in these chapters, but rather, only through allowing the various voices to operate "as if" they were one. In his essay on "Simplicities," William Gass, while trying to uphold the Shaker ideal of simplicity and extolling their sense of aesthetics, gradually reveals that when it comes to novelistic understanding, complexity and multiplicity have to be tamed into unity, but nonetheless have to express themselves. In a single gargantuan sentence, he tries to hold the insight in his mind.

Thinking how complex simplicity is, perhaps we have an answer. . . . Before the buzzing, blooming abundance of everyday life, facing the vast regions of ocean and the seemingly limitless stretches of empty space; or—instead— reading the novels of Henry James and James Joyce and Melville and Mann, or living in Proust or traveling in Tolstoy, you are again impressed by immensity, by the plethora of fact, by the static of statistics and the sheer din of data, by the interrelation of everything, by twists and turns and accumulations, as in this sentence going its endless way; yet as one proceeds in science, as one proceeds

through any complex aesthetic surface, as one proceeds,
the numerous subside in the direction of the few . . . the
power of numbers grasps vastness as though each Milky
Way were the sneeze of a cicada; so that slowly perhaps,
steadily certainly, simplicity reasserts itself. The simple sentence is achieved.

How, then, does one achieve this "simple sentence?" How does
one go about coordinating this triple voice of the authorial,
the narrative and the dramatic? Gass provides a clue in his classic short story about Midwestern life, "In the Heart of the Heart
of the Country." As a title character, Gass takes a nameless "I"
who occupies the position, as anthropologists would put it, of
a participant observer. His status in this Midwestern town, a
place referred to simply as "B," is something like that of the
ethnographer who travels to an exotic locale to live among the
"natives." Part of Gass's ingenuity, however, lies in turning the
lens back on us, so that we ourselves are the natives, and our
own habits and customs therefore get subjected to scrutiny.

   The idiosyncracies and the individual and collective beliefs
of this group of dwellers of "a small town fastened to a field in
Indiana" are held up for critical inspection. In this way, the
authorial voice, Gass's, known for its acerbic, perspicacious,
sometimes merciless qualities, positions itself at the center of
the story. Through his nameless character, on the surface somewhat detached, Gass endows this storyteller with the ability to
take the long view whenever it suits him. He even allows himself
the luxury of quoting documents from the past.

   In 1833, Colin Goodykoontz, an itinerant preacher
   with a name from a fairytale, summed up the situation in
   one Indiana town this way:
      "Ignorance and her squalid brood. A universal dearth
   of intellect. Total abstinence from literature is very generally practiced."

And yet, for all the isolation in which he lives, and the occasional dyspeptic pronouncements he allows himself, this narrator remains firmly ensconced in the life of the town. It would

not be accurate to state that he is in the town but not of it. On the contrary, this contemporary counterpart of Colin Goody-koontz, however literary he might wax, cannot entirely separate himself from the "squalid brood" of his neighbors. One of the means through which Gass ensures that his narrator will not doom himself to looking down on the townspeople from a lofty, irascible height is by making the story more about the narrator himself than it is about them. If any deep flaws are going to be revealed they will, in the end, be his flaws. This need dictates Gass's decision to tell the story in first person. And, because the character possesses qualities that we sense to be coming more or less directly from the authorial voice, this means that the author has chosen to make himself somewhat vulnerable by his personal investment in this character persona. Thus, the authorial voice and the dramatic voice work in tandem.

In part, Gass achieves this "simple sentence" effect through the way he structures "In the Heart of the Heart of the Country." The story consists of thirty-six brief vignettes, with subtitles that range from more "sociological" or "civic" ones ("Education," "Business,") to more personal ones ("My House, My Cat, My Company"). In essence, in these pages, the Rotary Club meets True Confessions. At every turn, the analytical voice (the authorial voice) blends with the more confessional one (the dramatic voice). Gass is not afraid to let authorial commentary give way to lyricism, sometimes with striking suddenness. For instance, the vignette entitled "Weather" reads as follows:

> In the Midwest, around the lower Lakes, the sky in the winter is heavy and close, and it is a rare day, a day to remark on, when the sky lifts and allows the heart up. I am keeping count, and as I write this page, it is eleven days since I have seen the sun.

The title leads us to expect a weather report, some sort of recitation of atmospheric conditions in this "small town fastened to a field in Indiana." But what the narrator seems most interested in is interior weather, his own, the climate of the downhearted emotional spell he is living through at the moment. The most important statistic given is that of the eleven days since "I have seen the sun." The phrasing includes a reference to his keeping notes—"as I write this page"—making us feel, in effect, that we're reading his diary entry, and are therefore privy to his private life. Here again, as we did in Colette's story "The Other Wife," we see the gossip effect at work, giving form to the dramatic voice, making it intimate and personal.

Confession and Detachment

This confessional vein doesn't keep the "I," however, from offering some pretty excoriating remarks about those small-town minds he is destined to live in the company of. That is because the authorial voice never disappears for long. Under the heading "People," this man lets fly a few less than charitable observations about the lackadaisical geezers he keeps tabs on in town.

> Along the street, delicately teetering, many grandfathers move in a dream. During the murderous heat of summer, they perch on window ledges, their feet dangling just inside the narrow shelf of shade the store has made, staring steadily into the street. Where their consciousness has gone I can't say. It's not in the eyes. Perhaps it's diffuse, all temperature and skin, like an infant's, though more mild.

Gass supplies us with a prickly travelogue, one that gives us an unsparing breakdown of the town's life as a whole, while also bringing us up close and personal. The use of the modifier "delicately" slips in a covert sympathy for these men who are being described as infantile. The fact that the action happens "in a dream" also makes the tableau more enticing. At first glance, the story might look like a guide or a manual, but the handling of language lets us know that it is fiction, plain and simple. The simultaneous workings of different levels of voice allow this dreamscape to have both fullness and texture. The narrative voice comes in precisely where the pretense of detachment starts to crumble away, the way stucco crumbles on a house in the Midwest long exposed to intemperate weather. Stucco, so suited to the desolate reaches of the Southwest, just won't serve in the blistering humidity of small-town Indiana, where you bake, then freeze, then live through thunderstorms, then drought.

Likewise, the authoritative and authorial voice of detachment, by itself, cannot serve Gass's ends as fictionist. What he wants to reveal is the woodwork beneath the facade, as well as the interior decoration—not of sanctimony—but of the sanctum sanctorum that is this narrator's soul. The narrator uses the kind of erudition and allusiveness that would be available to Gass, but always in service of opening the doors and windows of himself. He is not so much wearing his learning on his sleeve as he is wearing his heart on his sleeve.

The narrative voice works in concert with the other two levels of voice, so that he becomes at once authoritative and vulnerable, impermeable and permeable.

> I have met with some mischance, wings withering, as Plato says obscurely, and across the breadth of Ohio, like heaven on a table, I've fallen as far as the poet, to the sixth sort of body, this house in B, in Indiana, with its blue and gray bewitching windows, holy magical insides. Great thick evergreens protect its entry. And I live *in.*
>
> Lost in the corn rows, I remember feeling just another stalk, and thus this country takes me over in the way I occupy myself when I am well . . . completely—to the edge of both my house and my body. No one notices, when they walk by, that I am brimming in the doorways. My house, this place, and my body, I've come in mourning to be born in.

The use of the narrative voice allows this solitary speaker the freedom to "become" his house, through the power of an extended metaphor. A laid-back magic hovers at the story's borders. The narrative voice allows a haunting note of genteel gentleness to temper this man's steely exterior. In terms of technique, the skillful blending of authorial and dramatic voices lets the narrative voice become more supple, more subtle, more forgiving. This voice can begin to speak, without embarrassment or chagrin, of mourning and brimming and being lost in the corn rows. He can say that he is a house, and mean it, sort of, without getting all shamefaced about it.

Gass doesn't want to have his narrator come off as either maudlin or flinty. Either extreme would make the story's tone more monotonous, more *monos tonos*. He knows the inherent perils in writing about "the heartland." He wants to be able to explore fully his feelings about this literal and mental geography without succumbing either to the soft-focus, golden-light version of the Midwest, or the cheap, regional-bashing potshots of the tourist complainer. Negotiating the authorial, narrative and dramatic levels of voice in the way he does allows him to come up with a unique and personal appraisal. Voice allows him to erect "My House, This Place and Body" plank by plank, instead of forcing him to plunk down a pre-fab structure.

In trying to use these various levels of voice together, it may help you to choose as your narrator a character who occupies an insider-outsider status. This narrator might be someone new to a place, or someone who, while long a dweller there, feels emotionally separate from it. When William Faulkner put Quentin Compson and his roommate Shreve in a Harvard dorm, and had Quentin "tell about the South," he created not only human conflict, but a situation in which the multiple levels of voice could flourish. Quentin's now famous phrase "I don't hate the South," shows how rich with possibilities it is to create a character who has a love-hate relationship with the geography of his birth. Remember that the more you steep your character in his or her setting, the more knowledgable, passionate and ambivalent that character may turn out to be. Whether it's a clash of cultures, as in E.M. Forster's *A Passage to India*, or domestic differences between father and daughter, as in William Styron's *Lie Down In Darkness*, positioning your character on the edge of his or her world will locate you in the space where the different levels of voice clearly overlap.

GUILTY PLEASURES

Manuel Puig is another writer who understands the "simple sentence," the deceptive simplicity of voice that contains an artful complexity of syntax and vision. Puig, in the beginning, was not always taken as seriously as many of his Latin American counterparts of the novel, such as Mario Vargas Llosa, Guillermo Cabrera Infante and José Donoso. This initial critical disdain had much to do with the fact that Puig has always been an aficionado of pop culture—soap operas, B-movies, tango crooners. The truth is, none of us fiction writers can fully extricate ourselves from the kitsch in our lives. So what do we do with it? Some writers retain their pop tastes only as guilty pleasures. The genius of Puig was to turn those tastes into the centerpiece of his artistic process.

Mistakenly, some accused him of simply cannibalizing bad movies to make novels, but nothing could be further from the truth. What Puig did was to selectively parody the plots and themes of sentimental pop culture, all the while relying on classic fictional techniques and devices to create his comic, but ultimately much more sobering, effects. Puig's interweaving of authorial, dramatic and narrative voice lends authority to his fiction, and allows a reader to take in Puig's writing at a page-turner clip and still grasp his ambitious themes. His appealing use of voice makes his experimentation go down easy.

In an earlier chapter I spoke to you about a moviegoer named Binx Bolling, one of Walker Percy's creations. It turns out that modern, angst-ridden, Christian existentialists of the American South aren't the only people afflicted with an addiction to B-movies. Molina, one of the two main characters in Manuel Puig's *Kiss of the Spider Woman*, could probably relate to Binx's statement "I'm happy in a movie, even a bad movie." Just as for Binx, movies are more real for Molina than actual life. And in his case, it's probably a good thing, since real life consists of a prison cell.

There are some definite differences between them, though. Binx, a confirmed skirt-chaser, takes his cues about how to act in life from his macho mainstays William Holden and Rory Calhoun. Molina, on the other hand, is flamboyantly gay, and has his own unorthodox ideas about which movie idols are to be idolized. While Molina is telling his cellmate Valentin, a bona-fide political prisoner, the plot of a B-movie about a panther woman, Valentin asks him which of the characters he identifies with the most. Molina answers "With Irena, who do you think? She's the heroine, dummy. Always with the heroine."

Valentin and Molina are the ultimate odd couple, stranded in a jail cell together, one for revolutionary activities, the other for corrupting young boys. The only thing, in the beginning, that binds them together are the movie plots that Molina tells to pass the time. He exists as a kind of modern Latin American Scheherazade, helping pass the long days and nights through a contemporary brand of storytelling, always holding out the promise that more is to come. But although the lion's share of the book consists of dialogue, Puig does not simply write "movie-speak." He relies heavily on the dramatic voice, which we have defined as the voice in dialogue, but he anchors that voice with descriptive dream passages, playful psychological footnotes, and a report written by the uncomprehending prison detectives who keep Molina under surveillance.

FROM DRAMATIC TO NARRATIVE AND BACK

These other non-dialogue portions of the novel are weighted more heavily toward the narrative and authorial voices. They create a sense of fictional spaciousness around a dialogue-clotted jail cell that would otherwise feel claustrophobic and chatty. As readers, we are placed "in" the jail cell with Molina and Valentin, but Puig gives us enough room that we can interpret events through alternating voices.

One sequence of dialogue between the two men, for instance, is interrupted by Molina's telling of a movie plot. In the scene, animosity between the two cellmates has been building, but then starts to diffuse when the jailers poison the food of Valentin, so that he ends up with severe diarrhea as a result.

For the first time, we along with Molina, witness the vulnerable side of the iron-willed, stoic Valentin, who up until now has believed that it's "womanish" to show weakness of any kind. Molina, in turn, has a chance to nurture in the humble way he knows best, cleaning his cellmate's soiled body. Through this experience of acting as a good samaritan and compassionate fellow creature, he has his tenderness toward another accepted as something besides "queer" behavior.

Already, in the handling of dialogue, the so-called camera's eye has begun to betray that we are decidedly not sitting in a movie theater. Puig's complaint, in fact, about the movie that eventually was made of *Kiss of the Spider Woman* was that its cinematic imperatives ended up depicting Molina as in essence neurotic and unhappy, when Puig had conceived Molina as in essence joyous and compassionate.

> "But whatever you want, I'm the one who gets it for you. You don't budge."
> "And I promise not to laugh at your boleros anymore. I like the lyrics from that one you were singing before . . . they're okay."
> "I especially love the part that goes, '. . . and I wonder . . . could you be remembering too, sad dreams . . . of this strange love affair . . .' Divine, isn't it?"
> "You know what? I actually changed diapers on that poor comrade's baby boy, the guy they killed, I mean. We were all hiding out together in the same apartment, he and his wife, and their little son . . . Who knows what's to become of him now? He can't be more than three years old."

The selection of dialogue implies the emotional content of the scene—Valentin's reluctant acceptance, not only of his cellmate's ministrations, but also of the idiosyncracies of Molina's character—and his own. He begins to recover his revolutionary past, not in terms of clichés about "the struggle," but through the remembered image of himself taking care of a baby. Molina's evocation of the bolero about dreams and remembrance serves as a prompt for Valentin's own memory, allowing him to feel the kind of nourishing nostalgia that he has been denying himself up until this point.

The Hidden Author

This quality of dialogue begins to effect the reconciliation between Valentin's strict, stoical ideals of political commitment, which lack individual compassion, and Molina's personal loyalty within friendship, coupled with his excessive initial naïveté about the larger political world he lives in. Without any direct authorial commentary, Puig's novel nonetheless supplies more covert authorial interpretation. The interpretation is implied by the distance between the conversations in the bleak jail cell, and the fantasy world spun out from Molina's imagination, drawn from the plots of B-movies he has seen in the past, before he became a prisoner.

> —*a European woman, a bright woman, a beautiful woman, an educated woman, a woman with a knowledge of international politics, a woman with a knowledge of Marxism, a woman with whom it isn't necessary to explain it all from A to Z, a woman who knows how to stimulate a man's thinking with an intelligent question, a woman of unbribable integrity, a woman of impeccable taste . . .*

This deliciously melodramatic litany indicates the flighty mindset of Molina, who at this point in the evolution of his character can only understand political struggle in the hackneyed pop lingo of international intrigue. In his fantasy, a knowledge of Marxism and an impeccable fashion sense are given equal footing.

Even in the absence of a direct narrative voice, this switching of linguistic registers between one passage of the novel and the next forces us to read the different parts of the novel against one another. The above passage becomes especially significant later on in the novel, when the prison warden in fact attempts to bribe—or rather, to blackmail—Molina into cooperating with a plan to flush out Valentin's political comrades. Molina begins to discover the real and much less glamorous meaning of political intrigue when he has to decide where his loyalties lie.

In *Kiss of the Spider Woman*, the authorial voice exploits the contrast between the sections of dialogue in the prison cell (weighted toward the dramatic voice) and the narrated sections. In these narrated sections, Molina serves as the storyteller of movie plots, and Puig thereby provides us an idiosyncratic character voice and an implied narrator rolled into one. Molina isn't really a regular first-person narrator, because he restricts himself in these italicized passages to recounting preposterous plots with lots of embellishments. His "real" self does not exist within these creations, except as the storyteller, because what he is after is precisely to escape from himself and from the mundane circumstances of his prison. If anything, he wants to hold his real self in abeyance so he can indulge his flights of fancy.

His voice creates the effect of stories within the story. By alternating the emphasis between the dramatic and the narrative voice, from section to section, Puig can locate his character Molina either more inside the novel's political story or more outside it. Narrative technique reinforces the novel's theme of either facing up to one's identity and life circumstances, or using escapism and glittering fantasy to deny it. In one section Molina can tell one of his movie tales, and in the very next one, he can comment on his performance, or he and Valentin can quarrel about the relative social worth of Molina's stories. After Valentin makes a cutting remark, denigrating Molina's fantasies as childish and worthless, Molina vows not to recount any more plots aloud. But then when Valentine gets sick, he begs Molina to help him keep his mind off the pain by entertaining him with a plot. Molina, starting to relent and soften, says, "I swore I wouldn't tell you any more films. Now I'll go to hell for breaking my word."

Puig uses the clichés of popular culture and B-movies to explore very serious issues: friendship, sexuality, surviving psychic and physical torture, social justice, political commitment. Instead of offering us the stereotypes that populate movie plots, the novel ends up exploring human relationships with great complexity. The fluidity of Puig's multiple levels of voice makes it easier for him to make use of pop subject matter he cherishes without succumbing to the risk of "dumbing down" the novel.

DISCURSIVE AND DESCRIPTIVE

One of the bromides of writing workshops is "show, don't tell." This advice, however, flies in the face of how fiction writers actually work in combining levels of voice. A single work of fiction tends to vacillate between the discursive and descriptive voices. The descriptive voice has developed out of the emphasis of modern realistic fiction on rendering events in scene, so that we get to know a character, for instance, not through authorial commentary of her ideas, feelings and opinions, but rather through the setting she inhabits. Yet even those writers who try to adhere most strictly to the sheer descriptive voice will often find it necessary to interpolate phrases, sentences or entire paragraphs that offer a summary of what a character is feeling or thinking. The fact is, when the descriptive voice prevails in a strict and spartan fashion, one often ends up with boredom, as in the "camera's eye" novels of Alain Robbe-Grillet.

Knowing that the discursive voice—the voice of the commentator—will always creep into description, there's no reason why an author shouldn't make a virtue of necessity. Employing the discursive voice does not in any way imply bombast, as long as discursive qualities are not allowed to become too nakedly authorial. When the narrator takes the form of a well-defined protagonist speaking in the first person, as in David Bradley's *The Chaneysville Incident,* a writer can create dazzling effects with this multi-layered voice that far exceed what a more conventionally realistic, curtailed, restricted one could provide. And in using this multi-layered voice, one doesn't have to settle for anything less than sharp prose.

American fiction writers, on the whole, seem to have absolutely no qualms about creating character voices that are alcoholic, moronic, sophomoric or delusional, in search of a supposed psychological fidelity to the tortured psyche of the common man. The grittier the better. And yet, how timid most of us are about creating characters endowed with intelligence, eloquence, the capacity to analyze and reason as well as feel deeply. We give the keys to our homes to escaped convicts, in the vain hope of gleaning a little secondhand wastrel experience, but good God how we distrust eggheads. Heaven help us if our characters speak in complete sentences, let alone ones with subordinate clauses.

This reluctance stems from the deeply rooted anti-intellectualism of American writers—a trait not shared, on the whole, by writers of other countries. Consider the wide-ranging intellects of Milan Kundera and Mario Vargas Llosa, and the range of character voices featured in their novels. Then consider that they are the most popular novelists of their respective countries. Mario Vargas Llosa nearly won the presidency of his country at one time.

David Bradley is one American novelist daring enough to experiment with the full reach of character voice, embodied in John, the protagonist of *The Chaneysville Incident.* Like many a male in the American novel, John, a frustrated history graduate student, drinks hard. He takes his coffee black and his whisky neat. But unlike most of his counterparts, Bradley doesn't let John's liquid habit rob his power of speech. His hard-boiled bravado and the tang of his common phrases make him rank right up there with the best of those two-fisted novel stoics sitting atop a tightly corked keg of their own emotional pain. The initial dramatic sequence of the novel clips along predictably, if memorably, in the tough-talking lingo of a man whose world is about to come crashing down as soon as he recieves a telephone call announcing the death of his surrogate father.

Judith woke while I was making coffee. She had slept through the noise I had made showering and shaving and packing—she would sleep through Doomsday unless Gabriel's trumpet were accompanied by the smell of brewing coffee. She came into the kitchen rubbing sleep out of her eyes with both fists. Her robe hung open, exposing a flannel nightgown worn and ragged enough to reveal a flash of breast. She pushed a chair away from the table with a petulant thrust of hip, sat down in it, and dropped her hands, pulling her robe close with one, reaching for the mug of coffee I had poured for her with the other. She gulped the coffee straight and hot. I sat down across from her, creamed my own coffee, sipped it. I had made it strong, to keep me awake. I hated the taste of it.

Move over Raymond Chandler. And yet, Bradley doesn't content himself by simply continuing ad infinitum in this plainspoken vein, because he knows it would become tedious if he reined in the character voice to a litany of earthy and finally formulaic observations. Within a few pages, as John prepares to embark on a trip back to his childhood home to visit his ailing surrogate father, John as character/narrator launches into a long, pungent, disquisition on how you can understand class conflict in American society by contrasting the various modes of public transportation. His trenchant irony and exact vision make this discursive "essay" seem not an annoying digression, but a special pleasure. Ratcheting up to another level of voice—switching from a description-rich passage to a discourse-rich one—allows us to appreciate more fully the roots of John's rage against the world. Letting his mind become more spacious, through this use of the discursive voice, redeems him from seeming cramped and misanthropic. It also makes the novel feel roomier.

The key to the understanding of any society lies in the observation and analysis of the insignificant and the mundane. For one of the primary functions of societal institutions is to conceal the basic nature of society, so that the individuals that make up the power structure can pursue the business of consolidating and increasing their power untroubled by the minor carpings of a dissatisfied peasantry. . . .

Amerca's airports are built of plastic and aluminum. They gleam in the sun at noon, glow, at night, with fluorescent illumination. They are reached most conveniently by private autos, taxicabs, and "limousines." . . .

America's train stations are built of granite and brick, smoked and corroded from the pollution in city air. Their dim, cavernous hallways sigh of bygone splendor. They straddle that ancient boundary of social class—the legendary "tracks." . . .

America's bus stations tend to lurk in the section of town in which pornograhic materials are most easily obtained. Like airports, they are built of plastic, but it is plastic of a decidedly flimsier sort.

Room to Maneuver in the Attic

John compares the forms of transportation in everything from bar bourbon to architecture. What makes this "analysis" of American society interesting is that it embodies, finally, a personal complaint. John, naturally, rides the bus home. His elegant diatribes against whites in America remain complicated by the fact of his involvement in an interracial love relationship. When he ends up narrating the "Chaneysville Incident"—a massacre of slaves escaping through the Underground Railroad in Pennsylvania—he tells the story directly to his white girlfriend, who has a hand in deciphering its meaning for him. Because Bradley moves back and forth between personal and public, lyrical and analytical, descriptive and discursive, he deepens our understanding both of his protagonist and of the race-divided, class-stratified society in which John is compelled to live.

One of the most touching moments in the novel comes when John attends the funeral of his father, Moses Washington, and then ascends into Moses's attic, which lacks electricity, to read by lamplight a packet of documents left to him in the will. The packet contains his father's writings on one of his ancestors, killed in the Chaneysville incident. John inhabits a moment charged with personal confusion, not the least because of the conflictual relationship he'd had with his now-dead father. And yet, in a typical Bradley stylistic maneuver, the author doesn't allow the scene to simply become melancholy introspection. Rather than having the moment unfold in scenc (think of Emma Bovary in Flaubert's attic, reading her lover's upsetting letter), Bradley recasts this crucial moment as one of John's infamous mini-essays. Foregrounding the discursive voice, John, always the astute historian, cogitates on how the lamplight affects his first reading of this document that is about to change his life forever.

> Things look different in lamplight. That is a small fact, the kind of datum that escapes the notice of the average historian. . . . He misses the obvious—and therefore the significant—simply because he has never himself had to try and puzzle out the meaning of a text by the light of burning kerosene. . . . Could Franklin have written his "Essay on Populations" if he had had the unerring glow of incandescence showing up his bigotry? Was the only difference between *Plessy vs. Ferguson* and *Brown vs. the Board of Education of Topeka, Kansas* the fact that the former was written by lamplight and the latter under—probably—a fluorescent tube? Could the Kennedys have changed from Commie-hunters to liberals in the age of whale oil? Could King have penned that hopelessly naive letter from the Albany jail with a flickering candle forcing him to stop and think while the words steadied before his eyes? Could I puzzle out the truth better with a trouble light above my head, or perhaps a flashlight? . . .
>
> The attic was warmer now—warm enough to allow me to move my hands, pausing only occasionally to hold them above the lamp chimney. And so I put my hands on the folio, feeling the leather cool and smooth and worn beneath my hands. I slid my fingers along the flap, watching as the wax seal crumbled, bit by bit by bit.

These questions for John are not "academic." He has an intensely personal stake in trying to understand their consequences. He is trying to parse out his own subjectivity, his own penchant for misunderstanding, for holding grudges, for nourishing the willfully hostile feelings he harbors toward his father, even in death. Part of him, however, has started to be drawn to the remnants of his father's personal search into the past—a passion the two of them share, which makes them more alike than John would like to admit.

Wisely, Bradley modulates back into the descriptive voice in the final paragraph of this section of the novel, leaving us with a sensory image "as the wax seal crumbled, bit by bit by bit." The warmth of the attic brings us back into the intimacy and immediacy of the moment, reminding us that this novel is not about Franklin or King or the Kennedys but about John.

MERCURY

Never underestimate the intelligence of your readers. Don't make matters gratuitously difficult, but do allow your audience the pleasure of discovering how many ways a thing can be said, how many sides it can be seen from. Much of the beauty of voice lies in its manifold and ever-changing qualities. Writers tend to think of voice as air, transparent and clear. But voice is mercurial, in both senses of the word. Eloquent, shrewd, swift and thievish, like the god Mercury. And quick and changeable in character, like the element mercury.

For the fiction writer, an exhilaration comes from the knowledge that voice, our resource, our element, our medium, remains inexhaustible. The power to handle our viscous, volatile, sometimes poisonous element doesn't permit us to take its powers for granted. As in other forms of artistry, we have a deep and special reserve, in some respects peculiar to us, on which to draw. The element in our reserve, mercury, can be classified neither as a solid nor a liquid, but something in between.

The certain fact of this uncertain substance demands from us an almost scientific method and cunning. For despite my metaphor of an undifferentiated substance, our resource, in the end, is not a natural resource. We always have to be doing something with it, performing experiments, sticking it on the periodic table the better to analyze it: atomic number 80, atomic weight 200.59, melting point -38.87 degrees centigrade, boiling point 356.58 degrees centigrade, specific gravity 13.546, valences one and two. Or we dump its silvery white, toxic, metallic contents into a thermometer so that we can take frost readings through our bedroom window to determine whether we might just as well stay in bed.

As a boy, I remember sitting at home one ill-occupied Saturday morning, my idle hands the Devil's playthings, and starting to wonder about the fact that water had a much lower boiling point than mercury, so what would happen if I submerged the family thermometer in a pot of boiling water. Being an inquisitive sort, and not one to leave perfectly good hypotheses untested, I forthwith boiled some water and performed the experiment. As soon as the metal tip touched the boiling surface, the glass sheath cracked and the mercury shot straight out the top with volcanic speed. My parents were none too happy about having to replace the thermometer on account of my bone-headed curiosity. As punishment, I had to spend the whole morning in my room, repenting of my misdemeanor. What the heck. It was a small sacrifice to pay for art.

Exercises

1. Write a sketch narrated by a person isolated from his or her surroundings, but also intimate with them. Try to recreate the effect of the "simple sentences" of which Gass speaks. The narrator ought to be capable of both sharp critique and personal, lyrical introspecton. Make the voice both confessional and able to comment on his or her larger surroundings.

2. Use both the dramatic and narrative voices, in more or less equal proportion, in a story with a restrictive setting. The characters will have only dialogue available in relation to one another. Direct description should remain minimal. But you may explore other registers of the narrative voice such as reports, fantasy, diary entries, invented documents, to provide character context.

3. Create a story in which you give both the discursive and descriptive voice free rein. However, these two voices should exist within a single character, rather than splitting the task between character and narrator.

INDEX

Absalom, Absalom!, 148-153
Accent. *See* Dialect
Age of Iron, 26-27
"Algebra: A Problem With Words," 131-135
All the King's Men, 2
Ambassador's Son, The, 30-34
Anxiety of influence, 6
Aristotle, 146
Atmosphere: creating, 54-56; defined, 53; and tone, 5
Austin, Jane, 2-3
Author, and character, 65-67
Authorial voice, 178-180; and dialogue, tension between, 75-77; of detachment, 172-174
"Axolotl," 57-63

Babel, Isaac, 92-97
Barth, John, 68-70
Barthelme, Donald, 22-26
Book of Laughter and Forgetting, The, 65-67
Booth, Wayne, 76
Bradley, David, 180-185

Camus, Albert, 46-49
Centers of consciousness, 34-36, 39-40
Ceremony, 157-158
Chaneysville Incident, The, 180-185
Character: and author, 65-67; secondary, giving primary voice to, 123; sympathy for, and first-person narrators, 40-43
Character voice: consistency in, 25-27; and unreliable narrator, 45-49
Characters: in dialogue, 75-76; major vs. minor, 18-21
Cisneros, Sandra, 19-21
Coetzee, J.M., 26-28
Colette, 84-89
"Conversation With My Father, A," 79-81
Cortazar, Julio, 57-63

Death in Venice, 29-30
Delta Wedding, 54-56
Description: and dialogue, 17-18; discursive voice in, 180-183; tone of, 60-61
Devil in Disputanta, The, 136-140
"Di Grasso," 92-94
Dialect, 6; defined, 109; rendering, 100-102; varying, in same story, 105-108; and voice, balancing and unbalancing,

110-112. *See also* Folk speech; Speech, habits of
Dialogue, 3; as character backtalk, 79-81; and description, 17-18; dramatic voice within, 5-6; leisurely, allowing for, 81-84; and narrative restraint, 84-87; role of, within fiction, 74; script vs. fiction, 89-91; and single moment, 91-94. *See also* Character voice
Dramatic irony, 86-87

Emma, 2
Enormous Changes at the Last Minute, 41
Exercises, 28, 51, 73, 97, 117-118, 140, 162-163, 186; performing, 6-7

Faulkner, William, 62, 148-153
Fiction, "preachy", 77-79
Fiction of Reality, The, 144-146
First-person narration, 18, 43-45; and character sympathy, 40-43
Fitzgerald, F. Scott, 123
Flowers for Algernon, 62
Folk speech, 17, 21, 102
Folk tale, 16
Forster, E.M., 29
Fowles, John, 90
French Lieutenant's Woman, The, 90-91

Gass, William, 147-148, 169-174
Ghose, Zulfikar, 144-146
"Girl," 15-17
Gordon, Caroline, 88-89
Great Gatsby, The, 123

Hardy, Thomas, 24
Hemingway, Ernest, 158-161
House of Fiction, The, 88
Hurston, Zora Neale, 126-130

Imitation, and experience, 146-148
Implied author, 76
"In the Heart of the Heart of the Country," 170-174
Influence, and imitation, 6
Irony, 110-111; and voice, 30-34; dramatic, 86-87
Islas, Arturo, 158-162

James, Henry, 34-40
"Jilting of Granny Weatherall, The," 49-50

Johnny Got His Gun, 62
Johnson, Charles, 156-157
Jude the Obscure, 24

Kentuckiana, 70-73, 105-112
Keyes, Daniel, 62
Kincaid, Jamaica, 15-17
Kiss of the Spider Woman, 175-180
Kundera, Milan, 63-68, 70

Life and Opinions of Tristram Shandy, The,
    63-64
"Life Story," 68-70
"Little Miracles, Kept Promises," 19-21
Lolita, 123-125

Mann, Thomas, 29-30
"Master Time, A," 102-105
Mathews, Harry, 119
Metafiction: pure, drawbacks of, 68-70; and
    tone, 63-70
Mimetic faculty, defined, 146
Morris, Wright, 141-144
Moviegoer, The, 43-45
"My First Goose," 95-97

Nabokov, Vladimir, 123-125
Narrative authority, 5
Narrative restraint, and dialogue, 84-87
Narrator: achieving immediacy with, 49-50;
    and character sympathy, 40-43; first-
    person, 18, 43-45; omniscient, 70-71;
    third-person, 29-31, 33, 126; unreliable,
    and character voice, 45-49

Obscenity, use of, 115-117
Omniscient narrator, 70-71
On Being Blue, 147-148
"On the Steps of the Conservatory," 23-25
Oral History, 148-153
Originality, recognizing limits on, 145
"Other Wife, The," 85-88

Paley, Grace, 41-43, 79-81
Paragraphs, short, 85
Passage to India, A, 29
Percy, Walker, 43-45
Perfumes de Cartago, 12-15
Perkins, Owen, 131-135
Pinter, Harold, 90-91
Plot, 3; stock, new voice with, 135-140
Poetics, 146
Point of view, 29; and voice, 5; switching,
    49-51
Porter, Katherine Anne, 49-50
Portrait of a Lady, The, 34-40
Porzecanski, Teresa, 10-15, 120
Proust, Marcel, 76

Proverbs, and maxims, in speech, 16-17
Puig, Manuel, 175-180

Rain God, The, 160-162
Reading, as writer, 144-146
Remembrance of Things Past, 76
Rhetoric of Fiction, The, 76
Roberts, Elizabeth Maddox, 101-102

Sentence, simple, 169-175
Setting, choice of, 63
Silko, Leslie Marmon, 157-158
"Simplicities," 169-170
Smith, Lee, 148-153
"Snows of Kilamanjaro, The," 158-161
Sound and the Fury, The, 62
Speech: absurdist, 22; consistency in, 25-27;
    habits of, 5; plain, 17; sophisticated,
    110-112
Sterne, Laurence, 63-64
Still, James, 102-105
Stranger, The, 46-49
Style: choice of, in examples, 4; mechanics
    of, 112-117
Subject: defining, 119-120; finding, 6
Sympathetic characters, and first-person
    narrators, 40-43
Syntax, establishing inflections through,
    108-109

Tate, Allen, 88-89
Their Eyes Were Watching God, 126-130
Third-person narration, 29-31, 33, 126;
    achieving immediacy with, 49-50
Time of Man, The, 101-102
Tone: and atmosphere, 5; defined, 58; of
    description, 60-61; and metafiction,
    63-70; mock-epic, 70-71
Trumbo, Dalton, 62
Twenty Lines a Day, 119

Verbal mannerisms, 22-26
Vignettes, self-sufficient vs. self-contained,
    94-97
Voice: defined, 1-2; and dialect, balancing
    and unbalancing, 110-112; dramatic *(see*
    Dialogue); expansive, keeping control
    of, 126-127; individual, preserving
    inflections of, 108-110; and irony, 30-34;
    new, with stock plot, 135-140; primary,
    123-125; three levels of, 6; whimsical,
    132. *See also* Authorial voice, Character
    voice, Narrator
Voices, many: in concert, 164-166; speaking
    as one, 128-130

"Wants," 41-43
Waren, Robert Penn, 2-3
Welty, Eudora, 54-56